•Bar

ATLAS OF
TOWN PLANS

Bartholomew
An Imprint of HarperCollins*Publishers*

Published jointly by RAC Publishing, RAC House, Bartlett Street, South Croydon, CR2 6XW and Bartholomew, *an Imprint of* HarperCollins *Publishers*, 77-85 Fulham Palace Rd, Hammersmith, London W6 8JB

Created and typeset by West One (Trade) Publishing Ltd. for RAC Publishing.
Cartography by RAC Publishing.
Printed in Spain.

ISBN 0-7028-3081-X

Prepare for your journey

A few simple checks will reduce the likelihood of any problems arising on your journey.

● Battery - check connections to the terminals are clean and dry.

● Radiator - top up if necessary.

● Hose clips - check these are on tight.

● Fan belt - check it is in good condition.

● Wash/wipe - top up with screenwash, if necessary.

● Oil - is there enough in the engine?

● Lights - check all are working properly and

replace any broken bulbs.

● Windows - make sure these are clean, and wipers are working properly.

● Tyres - check the pressure is as recommended in your vehicle

handbook. Ensure the tread is at least 1.6mm across the width of

the tyre. Don't forget the spare.

● Keys - always carry a spare set.

Contents

Town Plans *Key*   4

List of Town Plans   5

Town Plans   6

London *West*   46

London *East*   47

London *M25*   49

The Channel Tunnel   79

Channel Ferry Ports   80

Town Plans *Key*

If you are visiting a city or town that you do not know, the first thing you need is a plan to help you find your way about, to show you where you can park, and to indicate the major buildings and sights.

Aberdeen
Dundee
Glasgow
Edinburgh
Newcastle upon Tyne
Belfast
Scarborough
Harrogate York
Blackpool Bradford Leeds Hull
Halifax Huddersfield
Manchester Stockport
Liverpool Sheffield
Chester Stoke-on-Trent
Dublin
Nottingham
Shrewsbury Telford Derby Leicester
Wolverhampton Peterborough Norwich
Birmingham Coventry
Northampton Cambridge
Stratford-upon-Avon
Cheltenham Milton Keynes Ipswich
Gloucester Oxford Colchester Harwich
Swansea Watford
Cardiff Bristol Reading □ LONDON Ramsgate
Bath Guildford Croydon Canterbury
Salisbury Winchester Folkestone Dover
Southampton Chichester
Exeter Bournemouth Portsmouth Brighton
Plymouth Torquay

Abbreviations

Avenue	Ave.	Green	Gn.
Boulevard	Blvd.	Lane	La.
Bridge	Br.	Parade	Pde.
Close	Cl.	Place	Pl.
Crescent	Cres.	Road	Rd.
Drive	Dr.	Square	Sq.
Embankment	Emb't.	Street	St.
Esplanade	Esp'de.	Terrace	Ter.
Gardens	Gdns.	Viaduct	V'duct.

Motorways
Throughroutes (one-way)
Other Roads
Restricted Roads
Pedestrian Roads
Footpaths
Shopping Area

Car Park (covered)
Car Park (open)
Tourist Information Centre
† Abbey/Cathedral
† Church
wc Public Convenience
Ⓜ Metro

Aberdeen	6	Leeds	42
Bath	7	Leicester	43
Belfast	8	Liverpool	44
Birmingham	10	London West	46
Blackpool	12	London East	47
Bournemouth	13	London M25	49
Bradford	14	Manchester	50
Brighton	15	Milton Keynes	52
Bristol	16	Newcastle upon Tyne	53
Cambridge	17	Northampton	54
Canterbury	18	Norwich	55
Cardiff	19	Nottingham	56
Cheltenham	20	Oxford	57
Chester	21	Peterborough	58
Chichester	22	Plymouth	59
Colchester	23	Portsmouth	60
Coventry	24	Ramsgate	61
Croydon	25	Reading	62
Derby	26	Salisbury	63
Dover	27	Scarborough	64
Dublin	28	Sheffield	65
Dundee	29	Shrewsbury	67
Edinburgh	30	Southampton	68
Exeter	31	Stockport	69
Folkestone	32	Stoke-on-Trent	70
Glasgow	33	Stratford-upon-Avon	71
Gloucester	34	Swansea	72
Guildford	35	Telford	73
Halifax	36	Torquay	74
Harrogate	37	Watford	75
Harwich	38	Winchester	76
Huddersfield	39	Wolverhampton	77
Hull	40	York	78
Ipswich	41		

Aberdeen

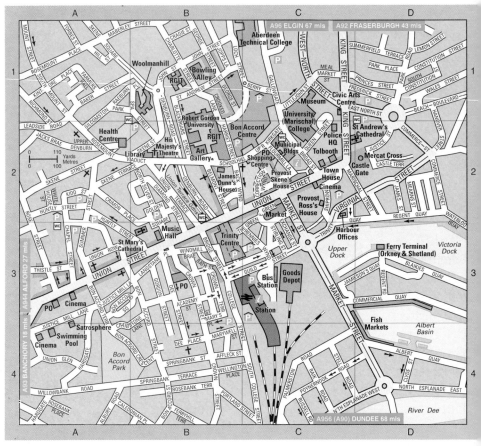

Academy St. B3
Affleck St. B4
Albert Quay D4
Albury Rd. A4
Back Wynd B2
Baker St. A1
Bath St. B3
Beach Blvd. D1
Belmont St. B2
Berry St. C1
Blackfriars St. B1/B2
Blakies Quay D3
Bon Accord Cres. A4/B4
Bon Accord Sq. A3
Bon Accord St. B3/B4
Bon Accord Ter. A3
Broad St. C2
Caledonian Pl. A4
Castle Ter. D2
Correction Wynd C2

Chapel St. A3
Charlotte St. B1
Clyde St. D4
College St. B3
Commerce St. D2
Commercial Quay D3
Constitution St. D1
Cragie St. B1
Craibstone La. A4/B3
Crimon Pl. A2
Crooked La. B1
Crown St. B3/B4
Crown Ter. B3
Dee Pl. B4
Dee St. B3
Denburn Rd. B2
Diamond St. B2
East Green C2
East North St. C1/D1
Exchange St. C3

Farmers Hall A1
Ferryhill Ter. B4
Flourmill La. C2
Forbes St. A1
Frederick St. D1
Gallowgate C1
George St. B1
Gilcomston Park A1
Golden Sq. B2
Gordon St. B3
Guild St. C3
Hanover St. D1/D2
Hardgate A4
Harriet St. B2
Hill St. A1
Huntly St. A2
Jacks Brae A2
James St. D2
Jamieson's Quay C3/D3

John St. B1
Jopps La. B1
Justice Mill La. A3
Justice St. D2
Kidd St. A2
King St. C1/C2
Kintore Pl. A1
Langstane Pl. B3
Leadside Rd. A2
Lemon St. D1
Little John St. C1
Loch St. B1
Maberley St. A1/B1
Market St. C2/D4
Marywell St. B4
Meal Market St. C1
Mearns St. D2
Mount St. A1
North Esp'de East D4
North Esp'de West C3

North Silver St. B2
Palmerston Rd. C4
Park Pl. D1
Park Rd. D1
Portland St. B4/C4
Poynernook Rd. C4
Princes St. D1
Queen St. C2
Raeburn Pl. A1
Raik Rd. C4
Regent Quay D2
Regent Rd. D3
Rennes Wynd C3
Richmond St. A1
Rose St. A2/A3
Rosebank Pl. A4
Rosebank Ter. B4
Rosemount Pl. A1
Rosemount V'duct. A2
Russell Rd. C4

St. Andrew St. B1
St. Mary's Pl. B3
School Hill B2
Shiprow C2
Skene Sq. A1
Skene St. A2
Skene Ter. A2
South College St. C4
Sth Constitution St. D1
South Mount St. A1
Springbank St. B4
Springbank Ter. B4
Stell Rd. C4
Stirling St. C3
Summer St. A2/A3
Summerfield Ter. D1
The Green C3
Thistle St. A3
Trinity Quay C3
Union Glen A4

Union Row A3
Union St. A3/C2
Union Ter. B2
Upper Denburn A2
Upper Kirkgate C2
Virginia St. C2
Wales St. D1
Waterloo Quay D2
Wellington Pl. B4
West North St. C1
White House St. A2
Willowbank Rd. A4
Windmill Brae B3
Woolmanhill B1/B2

Bath

Town plan see page 7

Abbey Gn. C3
Abbeygate St. C3
Alfred St. B1
Ambury St. B4
Amery La. B3

Archway St. D4
Avon St. B3
Bartlett St. B1
Barton St. B2
Bath St. B3

Bathwick St. D1
Beau St. B3
Beaufort Sq. B2
Bennett St. B1
Bridge St. C2

Bristol Rd. A4
Broad Quay B4
Broad St. B2
Broadway D4
Brock St. A1

Catherine Pl. A1
Chapel Row A2
Charles St. A3
Charlotte St. A2
Cheap St. C3

6

Bath

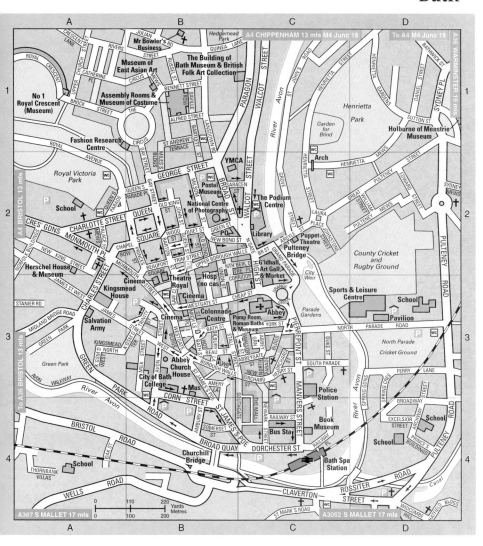

continued from page 6

Circus Mews B1
Claverton St. C4
Corn St. B4
Crescent Gdns. A2
Crescent La. A1
Daniel St. D1
Dorchester St. C4
Duke St. C3
Edward St. D2
Excelsior St. D4
Ferry La. D3
Gay St. B2
George St. B2
Grand Parade C2
Great Pulteney St. D2

Green Park A3
Green Park Rd. A3
Green St. B2
Grove St. C2
Guinea La. B1
Hatfield Buildings D4
Henrietta Gdns. D1
Henrietta Mews C2
Henrietta St. C1
Henry St. C3
High St. C2
Hot Bath St. B3
James St. West A3
Johnstone St. C2
Julian St. B1

Kingsmead North A3
Kingsmead Ter. B3
Kingsmead West A3
Lansdown Rd. B1
Laura Pl. C2
Lwr Boro' Walls B3
Manvers St. C4
Midland Br. Rd. A3
Miles's Buildings B2
Milk St. B3
Milsom St. B2
Monmouth Pl. A2
Monmouth St. A2
Northgate St. C2
N'thumberland Pl. B2

Newark St. C4
New Bond St. B2
New King St. A2
New Orchard St. C3
Norfolk Buildings A2
North Parade
  Buildings C3
Oak St. A4
Old Bond St. B2
Old King St. B2
Orange Grove C3
Orchard St. C3
Palace Yard Mews A2
Paragon C1
Pierrepont St. C3
Prince's Buildings D4
Princes St. B2

Pulteney Mews D2
Pulteney Rd. D2/D4
Queen Sq. B2
Queen St. B2
Queens Parade A2
Queens Parade Pl. B2
Quiet St. B2
Railway Pl. C4
Railway St. C4
Rivers St. A1/A2
Rossiter Rd. D4
Royal Av. A1/A2
Royal Cres. A1
Russel St. B1
St. Andrew's Ter. B1
St. James's Pde. B4
St. Johns Rd. C1

St. Mark's Rd. C4
St. Michael's Pl. B3
Saracen St. B2
Saville Row B1
Saw Close B3
Slow St. C3
South Parade C3
Southgate C4
Spring Cres. D3
Spring Gdns. D4
Stall St. B3
Stanier Rd. A3
Sutton St. D1
Sydney Mews D2
Sydney Pl. D1
The Circus B1

The Corridor C3
The Mall C4
Thornbank Villas A4
Tilbury La. B3
Trim St. B2
Trinity St. B3
Union St. B2
Upr Boro' Walls B2
Upper Church St. A1
Walco St. C1/C2
Wells Rd. A4
Westgate Buildings B3
Westgate St. B3
Widcombe Hill D4
William St. D2
Wood St. B2
York St. C3

Belfast

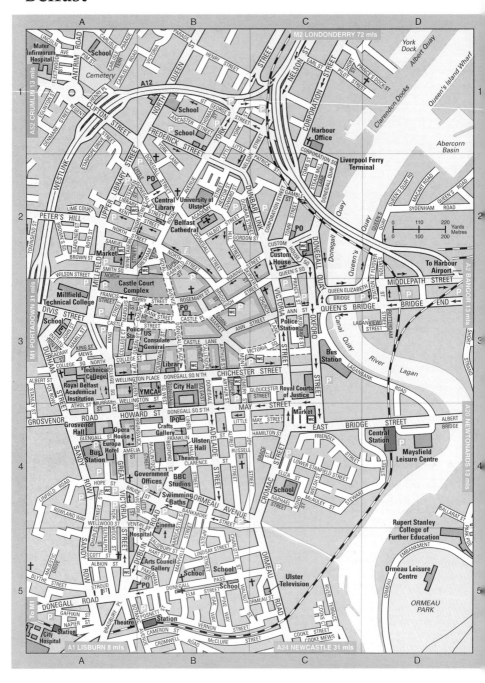

Belfast

Academy St. B2
Adelaide St. B4
Albert Br. D4
Albert St. A3
Albion St. A5
Alfred St. B4
Amelia St. A4
Ann St. B3/C3
Antrim Rd. A1
Apsley St. B4
Arthur St. B3
Athol St. A4
Ballarat St. D4
Bank St. B3
Bankmore St. B4
Bedford St. B4
Berry St. B3
Blythe St. A5
Bond St. C4
Botanic Ave. A5
Boyd St. A2
Bradbury Pl. A5
Bridge End D3
Bridge St. B3
Brown St. A2
Brown's Sq. A2
Bruce St. A4
Brunswick St. B4
Callender St. B3
Cameron St. B5
Carlisle Pde. A1
Carlisle Rd. A1
Carlisle Ter. A1

Castle La. B3
Castle Pl. B3
Castle St. A3
Chapel La. B3
Charles St. South A5
Charlotte St. B5
Chichester St. B3
Church La. C3
Clarence St. B4
Clifton St. A1
College Court A3
College Sq. East A3
College Sq. North A3
College St. A3
Cooke Court C5
Cooke Mews C5
Cooke St. C5
Copeland St. B5
Cornmarket B3
Corporation Sq. C1
Corporation St. C2
Cromac St. C4
Cromwell Rd. B5
Custom House Sq. C2
Dalton St. D2
Denmark St. A1
Divis St. A3
Donegall Pass B5
Donegall Pl. B3
Donegall Quay C2
Donegall Rd. A5
Donegall Sq. East B3
Donegall Sq. North B3

Donegall Sq. South B4
Donegall Sq. West B3
Donegall St. B2
Dublin Rd. B5
Dunbar Link C2
Dunbar St. B2
Durham St. A3
Earl St. C1
East Bridge St. C4
Edward St. B2
Eglinton St. A1
Eliza St. C4
Elm St. B5
Fleetwood St. A1
Fountain St. B3
Fox Row A3
Francis St. A3
Franklin St. B4
Frederick St. B1
Friendly St. C4
Gaffikin St. A5
Galway St. A3
Gamble St. C2
Gardiner St. A2
Glenalpin St. A5
Glengall St. A4
Gloucester St. C3
Gordon St. B2
Grace St. C4
Great George's St. B1/C1
Great Victoria St. A4
Gresham St. B2

Grosvenor Rd. A4
Hamill St. A3
Hamilton St. C4
Hardcastle St. B5
Hart St. B5
Hector St. B2
Henry Pl. A1
Henry St. B1
High St. B3
Hill St. B2
Hope St. A4
Howard St. A4
Institution Pl. A3
John St. A3
Joy St. B4
Kent St. A2
King St. Mews A3
King St. A3
Laganbank Rd. C3
Laganview St. D3
Lancaster St. B1
Library St. A2
Lime Court A2
Lincoln Ave. A1
Lindsay St. B5
Linen Hall St. B4
Linfield Rd. A4
Little Donegall St. B2
Little May St. B4
Little Patrick St. B1
Little Victoria St. B4
Little York St. B1
Lower Stanfield St. C4

Macart Rd. D2
Majestic Dr. A5
Marquis St. A3
Maryville St. B5
May St. B4
McAuley St. C4
McClintock St. B4
McClure St. B5
Middlepath St. D3
Millfield A2
Montgomery St. B3
Murray St. A3
Musgrave St. C3
Napier St. A5
Nelson St. B2/C1
North Queen St. B1
North St. A2/B2
Norwood St. A4
Oak Way B5
Ormeau Ave. B4
Ormeau Embankment D5
Ormeau Rd. C5
Ormeau St. C5
Oxford St. C3
Pakenham St. B5
Park Pde. D5
Peter's Hill A2
Pilot St. C1
Pim St. A1
Pine Way B5
Postnett St. B5
Prince's Dock St. C1

Prince's St. C3
Queen Elizabeth Br. C3
Queen St. A3
Queen's Br. C3
Queen's Quay Rd. D2
Queen's Quay D2
Queen's Rd. D2
Queen's Sq. C2
Raphael St. C4
Regent St. A1
River Ter. C5
Rosemary St. B3
Rotterdam St. D3
Rowland Way A4
Royal Ave. B2/3
Russell St. B4
Salisbury St. B5
Samuel St. A2
Sandy Row A4/5
Scott St. A5
Scrabo St. D2
Short Strand D3
Short St. C1
Skipper St. B2
Smith Sq. North A2
Stanhope Dr. A2
Stanley St. A3
Station St. D2
Station St. Flyover D3
Steam Mill La. C2
Stephen St. A2
Stewart St. C4
Stroud St. A5

Sydenham Rd. D2
Talbot St. B2
Thomas St. B1
Tomb St. C2
Townsend St. A2
Union St. A2
Upper Arthur St. B3
Upper Garfield St. B2
Upper Library St. A2
Upper Queen St. A3
Vernon St. B5
Ventry St. A4
Victoria Pde. B1
Victoria Sq. C3
Victoria St. C3
Walnut St. B5
Waring St. B2
Wellington Pl. A3
Wellington St. A3
Wellwood St. A4
Welsh St. C4
Westlink A2
Wilson St. A2
Wine Tavern St. A2
York La. B1
York St. B1

Motoring and the Environment

Take a few simple measures to minimise the impact of your car on the environment and you'll also make significant savings in motoring costs.

- Choose your car with care, taking into account type of fuel, fuel consumption and engine size.
- Ensure your car is regularly serviced.
- Avoid heavy acceleration and braking.
- Keep within the speed limits.
- Select the right gear, getting into the highest gear as soon as possible.
- Don't carry unnecessary loads, and remove roof-racks when not in use.
- Avoid congestion wherever possible.
- Switch off the engine in severe traffic jams.
- Use public transport when possible.

9

Birmingham

Index see opposite page

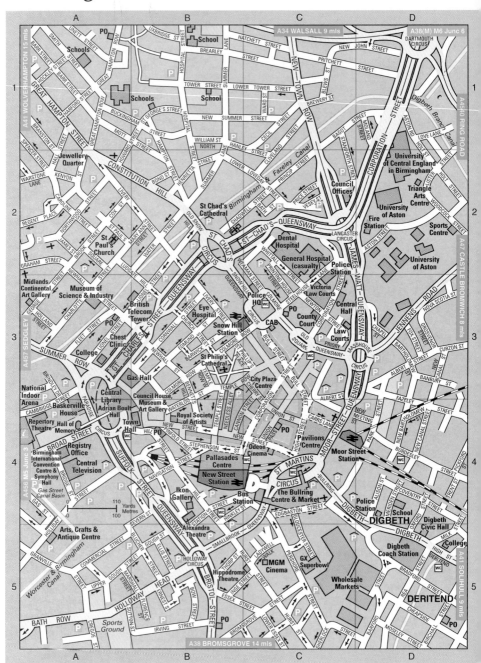

10

Birmingham *Index*

Albert St. C3/C4
Alison St. D4
Aston Rd. D1
Aston St. D2
Bagot St. C1
Banbury St. D3
Barford St. D5
Barr St. A1
Bartholomew St. D3
Barwick St. B3
Bath Row A5
Bennetts Hill B3/B4
Birchall St. D5
Blews St. C1
Blucher St. B5
Bordesley St. D4
Bow St. B5
Bradford St. D5
Branston St. A1
Brearley St. B1
Brewery St. C1
Bridge St. A4
Brindley Dr. A3
Bristol St. B5
Broad St. A4

Bromsgrove St. B5/C5
Brook St. A2
Buckingham St. A1/B1
Bull St. C3
Bullring C4
Cambridge St. A4
Cannon St. B4
Caroline St. A2
Carrs La. C4
Cecil St. C1
Chapel St. D3
Charlotte St. A3
Cheapside D5
Church St. B3
Colmore Circus C3
Colmore Row B3
Commercial St. A5
Cornwall St. B3
Corporation St. C4/D1
Coventry St. D4
Cox St. A2
Cregoe St. A5
Curzon St. D3
Digbeth D5
Edgbaston St. C4

Edmund St. B3
Ellis St. B5
Ernest St. B5
Essex St. B5
Fazeley St. D3/D4
Fleet St. A3
Florence St. B5
Fox St. D3
Gas St. A4
George St. A3
Gloucester St. C4/C5
Gough St. B5
Graham St. A2
Granville St. A5
Gt Charles St. Q'way B3
Great Hampton St. A1
Hall St. A1/A2
Hampton St. B1/B2
Hanley St. B1/C2
Hatchett St. B1/C1
Henrietta St. B2
High St. C4
Hill St. B4
High St. (Deritend) D5

Hinkley St. B4
Hockley St. A1
Holland St. A3
Holliday St. A4/A5
Holloway Head A5/B5
Holt St. D2
Hospital St. B1
Howard St. A2
Hurst St. C5
Inge St. B5
Irving St. B5
James St. A2
James Watt Q'way D3
Jennens Rd. D3
Kenyon St. A2
Ladywell Walk C5
Lancaster Circus C2
Lionel St. A3/B3
Lister St. D2
Livery St. A2/B3
Love La. B1
Lower Loveday St. B2/C2
Lower Tower St. B1/C1

Marshall St. A5
Masshouse Circ. C3/D3
Meriden St. D4
Milk St. D5
Moor St. Q'way C4
Moseley St. D5
Mott St. A1/B1
Navigation St. B4
Needles Alley B4
New St. B4
New Bartholomew St. D4
New Canal St. D4/D3
New John St. C1/D1
New Meeting St. D4
Newhall St. A3/B3
Newton St. C3
Northwood St. A2
Nova Scotia St. D3
Old Snow Hill B2
Old Sq. C3
Oxford St. D4
Paradise Circus A3/A4
Park St. D4
Pershore St. C5
Pickford St. D4

Pinfold St. B4
Price St. C2
Princip St. C2
Printing House St. C2/C3
Priory Q'way C3
Pritchett St. C1/D1
Rea St. D5
Regent Pl. A2
St Chad's Circus B2
St George's St. B1
St Martin's Circus C4
St Paul's Sq. A2
St Phillip's Pl. B3
Severn St. B4
Shadwell St. B2/C2
Sherlock St. C5
Smallbrook Q'way B5
Smith St. A1
Snowhill Q'way B3
Spencer St. A1/A2
Stanforth C1/C2
Station St. B4
Steelhouse La. C3
Stephenson St. B4

Suffolk St. Q'way A4/B4
Summer La. B1/B2
Summer Row A3
Sutton St. A5
Temple Row B3
Temple Row West B3
Temple St. B4
Thorp St. B5
Tower St. B1
Trent St. D4
Unett St. A1
Union Pass C4
Union St. C4
Upper Gough St. A5
Uxbridge St. B1
Vesey St. C2
Warstone La. A2
Water St. B2
Waterloo St. B4
Weaman St. C2/C3
Whittall St. C2
William St. North B1
Woodcock St. D2

Safety in Town

- When driving at night, always stick to main, well-lit roads.
- Lock all your doors when driving in urban areas and at low speeds.
- Don't leave valuables such as wallets and cameras on the passenger seat.
- Don't pull up too close to the car in front, you may need to take evasive action.
- If you are rammed or are being followed, don't stop. Drive straight to the nearest police station or brightly lit, busy area. Sound your horn and flash your lights to attract attention.
- If you see another driver in difficulty, drive on and report it by telephone as soon as you are able.
- Always lock your vehicle, even if you are only leaving it for a few minutes.
- Security mark your stereo or take it with you if it's removable.
- Always try to park in a well-lit area.

11

Blackpool

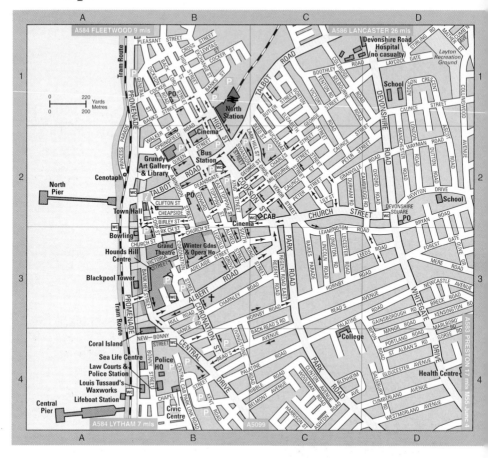

Abingdon St. B2	Buchanan St. C2	Coronation St. B3	Gainsborough Rd.	Leeds Rd. C3/D3	Olive Grove D3	Salisbury Rd. D4
Addison Cres. D1	Butler St. C1	Corporation St. B2	D3	Leicester Rd. C3	Oxford Rd. D2	Seed St. C2
Adelaide St. B3	Cambridge Rd. D2	Cross St. B1	General St. B1	Leopold Grove B3	Palatine Rd. C4/D3	Selbourne Rd. C1
Albert Rd. B3	Caunce St. C2/D1	Cumberland Ave.	George St. B2/C1	Lewtas St. B1	Park Rd. C3/4	South King St.
Alfred St. B3	Central Dr. B4	D4	Gloucester Ave. D4	Lily St. C2	Peter St. C2	B3/C3
Ascot Rd. D2	Central Car Pk Link	Deansgate B2	Gorse Rd. D4	Lincoln Rd. C3	Pleasant St. B1	Springfield Rd. B2
Ashton Rd. C4	Rd. B4	Devonshire Rd.	Gorton St. C1	Livingstone Rd. B4	Portland Rd. D4	Stirling Rd. D1
Back Church St. B3	Chapel St. B4	D1/2	Granville Rd. C2	London Rd. D2	Princess Pde. A2	Swanson St. B2
Back Lord St. B1	Charles St. C2	Devonshire Sq. D2	Grosvenor St. C2	Longton Rd. C3	Promenade	Talbot Rd. B2/C1
Back Read's Rd. C4	Charnley Rd. B3	Dickson Rd. B1	Harrison St. C4	Manchester Rd. D2	A1/2/3/4	Topping St. B2
Bank Hey St. B3	Cheapside B2	Durham Rd. C2	High St. B1/2	Manor Rd. D3/4	Queen St. B2	Vance Rd. B4
Banks St. B1	Church St. B3/C2	Dutton Rd. D2	Hornby Rd. B3/ C3	Marlborough Rd.	Raikes Pde. C3	Victoria St. B3
Belmont Ave. C4	Clifton St. B2	East Topping St.	Hull Rd. B3	D3	Read's Ave.	Victory Rd. C1
Birley St. B2	Clinton Ave. C4	B2	Kensington Rd. D3	Mather St. D1	B4/C3/D3	Walker St. B2
Blenheim Ave. C4	Cocker St. B1	Edward St. B2	Kent Rd. B4	Mere Rd. D3	Regent Rd. C3	Wayman Rd. D2
Bonny St. B4	Coleridge Rd. C1	Elizabeth St. C1/2	King St. B2	Milbourne St. C2	Regent Rd. East C3	Westmorland Ave.
Boothley Rd. C1	Collingwood Ave.	Exchange St. B1	Lark Hill St. C2	New Bonny St. B4	Ribble Rd. C4	D4
Breck Rd. D3	D1/2	Fenton Rd. C1	Laycock Gate D1	Newcastle Ave. D3	Ripon Rd. D4	Whitegate Dr. D3/4
Bryan Rd. D2	Cookson St. B2	Forest Gate D3	Leamington Rd. C3	Newton Dr. D2	St Alban's Rd. D4	Woolman Rd. C4

Bournemouth

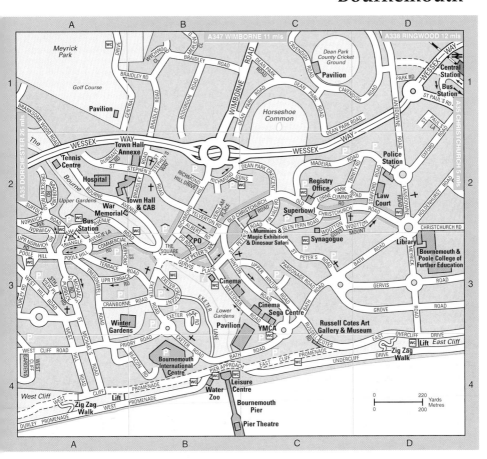

Albert Rd. B2	Commercial Rd. A3	Exeter Park Rd. B3	Meyrick Rd. D3	Richmond Gdns. B2	Suffolk Rd. A2	West Cliff Prom'de. A4/B4
Avenue La. A3	Cranborne Rd. A3	Exeter Rd. B3	Norwich Ave. A2	Richmond Hill. B2	Terrace Rd. A3	West Cliff Rd. A4
Avenue Rd. A2	Crescent Rd. A2	Fir Vale Rd. C2	Norwich Rd. A2	Richmond Hill Dr. B2	The Square. B3	West Hill Rd. A3/A4
Bath Rd. B4/D3	Cumnor Rd. C2	Gervis Pl. B3	Old Christ'ch Rd. B2/D2	Richmond Rd. C3	The Triangle A3	West Prom'de. A4/B4
Beacon Rd. B4	Dean Park Cres. C2	Gervis Rd. D3	Orchard St. A3	Russell-Cotes Rd. C3	Tregonwell Rd. A3	Westover Rd. B3
Bodorgon Rd. B1	Dean Park Rd. C1	Glen Fern Rd. C2	Oxford Rd. D2	St. Michael's Rd. A3/A4	Trinity Rd. C2	Wimborne Rd. B1
Bourne Ave. A2	Durley Prom'de. A4	Grove Rd. D3	Park Rd. D1	St. Paul's La. D1	Undercliff Dr. C4/D4	Wootton Gdns. C2
Bradburn Rd. A2	Durley Rd. A3	Hinton Rd. B3	Parsonage Rd. C3	St. Paul's Rd. D1	Upr Hinton Rd. C3	Wootton Mount D2
Braidley Rd. B1/B2	Durrant Rd. A2	Holdenhurst Rd. D2	Pier Approach B4	St. Peter's Rd. C3	Upr Norwich Rd. A3	Wychwood Cl. B1
Branksome Wood Rd. A1	East Cliff Prom'de. C4	Lansdowne Rd. D1/D2	Poole Hill A3	St. Peter's Walk B3	Upr Terrace Rd. A3	Yelverton Rd. B2
Cavendish Rd. C1	East Overcliff Dr. D4	Lorne Park Rd. C2	Post Office Rd. B3	St. Stephen's Rd. A2	Verulam Pl. B2	
Central Dr. A1	Exeter Cres. B3	Madeira Rd. C2	Priory Rd. A4	St. Stephen's Way. B2	Wessex Way A2/D1	
Christchurch Rd. D2	Exeter La. B3	Merlewood Cl. B1	Purbeck Rd. A3	Stafford Rd. D2	West Cliff Gdns. A4	

Bradford

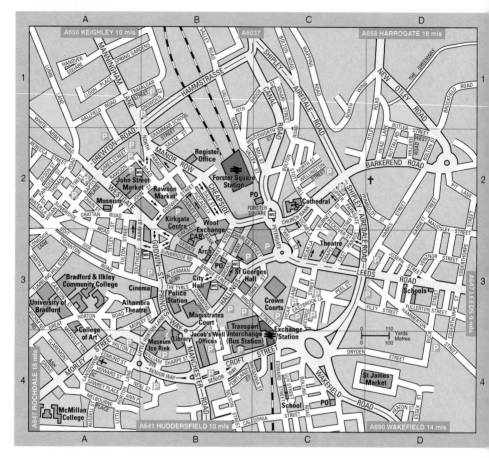

Aldermanbury B3	Channing Way B3	Forster Sq. C2	Holdsworth St. C2	Neal St. A4	Salem St. B2	Valley Rd. B1
Ann Pl. A4	Chapel St. C3	Fullerton St. D3	Howard St. A4	Nelson St. B4	Sawrey Pl. A4	Valley St. B2
Ash Grove A4	Charles St. B3	Fulton St. A3	Humboldt St. D2	New Otley Rd. D1	Senior Way B4	Ventnor St. D3
Bank St. B3	Cheapside B2	Garnett St. D2	Ivegate B3	North Brook St. B1	Sharpe St. B4	Vicar La. C2/3
Baptist Pl. A2	Church Bank. C2	George St. C3	John St. A2	North Parade B2	Shipley-Airdale Rd.	Wakefield Rd. C4
Barkerend Rd. D2	Claremont A4	Godwin St. B2/3	Joseph St. D3	North St. C2	C1/2	Wapping Rd. C1
Barry St. A3	Croft St. B4	Goit Side A3	Kirkgate B3	North Wing C1	Simes St. A2	Water La. A2
Bolling Rd. C4	Dale St. B2	Grammar School St.	Lansdowne Pl. A4	Nuttall Rd. D2	Smith St. A3	Well St. C3
Bolton Rd. C1/2	Darley St. B2	B2	Leeds Rd. C/D3	Otley Rd. D2	Snowden St. B1	Wellington St. C2
Bolton St. D2	Drake St. C3	Grattan Rd. A2	Little Horton La. A4/B3	Paradise St. A2	Southgate A3	Westgate A2
Bridge St. B3	Drewton Rd. A2	Great Horton Rd. A3	Longside La. A3	Peckover St. C2	Spring Gdns. A1	Wharf St. C1
Britannia St. C4	Dryden St. C4	Guy St. C4	Lumb La. A1	Peel St. C3	St Thomas Rd. A2	White Abbey Rd. A1
Broadway B3	Dyson St. A2	Halfield Rd. A1	Manchester Rd. B4	Petergate C3	Stott St. C2	Wigan St. A3
Brookfield Rd. D1	East Pde. C3	Hallings B3	Manningham La. A1	Piccadilly B2	Sunbridge Rd. A2/B3	William St. B4
Buck St. D4	Eastbrook La. C3	Hammerton St. D3	Manor Row B2	Pit La. C1	Tetley St. A3	Wilton St. A4
Burnett St. C2	Edderthorpe St. D3	Hammstrasse B1	Manville Ter. A4	Portland St. B4	The Greenway D1	
Butler Street West. D1	Edmund St. A4	Hanover Square A1	Market St. B3	Princes Way B3	The Tyrls B3	
Caledonia St. B4	Edward St. C4	Harris St. D2	Maudsley St. D2	Rawson Rd. A2	Thornton Rd. A3	
Canal Rd. C1	Eldon Pl. A1	Head La. D2	Melbourne Pl. A4	Rebecca St. A2	Trafalgar St. A1	
Carlton St. A3	Essex St. D4	Heaton St. D4	Mill St. C2	Richmond Rd. A3	Tumbling Hill St. A3	
Chain St. A2	Filey St. D3	Hillside Rd. D2	Morley St. A4	Russell St. A4	Upper Parkgate C2	

Brighton

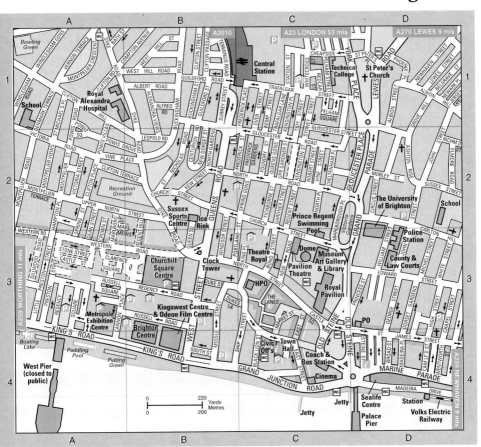

Albert Rd. B1	Circus St. D2	Gardner St. C2	Little Preston St. A3	North St. C3	Russell Rd. B3	Upper Gardner St. C2
Albion Hill D1	Clarence Sq. A3	George St. D3	Madeira Dr. D4	Old Steine C4	Russell Sq. A3	Upper North St. A2
Albion St. D1	Clifton Hill A1	Gloucester Pl. D2	Madeira Pl. D4	Over St. C1	Ship St. B4	Vernon Ter. A1
Alexandra View B1	Clifton Passage B1	Gloucester Rd. C2	Marine Pde. D4	Pelham Sq. C1	Sillwood Rd. A3	Victoria Rd. A2
Alfred Rd. B1	Clifton Pl. A2	Gloucester St. C2	Market St. C3	Pelham St. C1	South St. B4	Victoria St. A2
Ashton Rise D2	Clifton Rd. A1	Grand Junction Rd. C4	Marlborough Mews A2	Phoenix Pl. D1	Spring Gdns. C2	Vine Pl. A2
Bath St. A1	Clifton St. B1	Grand Pde. D2	Marlborough Pl. C2	Portland St. B3	Spring St. A2	Vine St. C2
Belgrave St. D1	Clifton Ter. A2	Grove Hill C3	Marlborough St. A2/A3	Powis Grove A2	St. James St. D4	Wentworth St. D4
Black Lion St. C4	Compton Ave. B1	Guildford Rd. B1	Michell St. D3	Powis Rd. A2	St. Michael's Pl. A1	West Hill Rd. B1
Bond St. C3	Crown St. A2A/3	Guildford St. B1	Middle St. B4	Powis Sq. A1/A2	St. Nicholas Rd. B2	West Hill St. B1
Broad St. D4	Dean St. A2/A3	Hampton Pl. A2	Montpelier Cres. A1	Powis Villas A2	St. Peter's Pl. D1	West St. B3
Buckingham Rd. B1	Denmark Ter. A1	High St. D3	Montpelier Rd. A2	Preston St. A3	Station St. C1	Western Rd. A3/B3
Buckingham St. B1	Dorset Gdns. D3	Jersey St. D1	Montpelier St. A2	Princess St. D3	Steine St. D4	White St. D3
Camelford St. D4	Duke St. B3	John St. D2/D3	Montpelier Ter. A2	Queen Sq. B3	Stone St. A3	Whitecross St. C1
Cannon Pl. A3	Dukes La. B3	Kemp St. C1	Montpelier Views A2	Queens Gdns. C2	Surrey St. B1	William St. D3
Carlton St. D3	Dyke Rd. A1/B2	Kensington Pl. C1	Morley St. D2	Queens Rd. B2	Sussex St. D2	Windlesham Gdns. A1
Castle Sq. C3	East St. C3/4	Kensington St. C2	New Dorset St. B2	Redcar St. C1	Sydney St. C1/C2	Windlesham Rd. A1
Castle St. A3	Edward St. D3	Kew St. B2	New Rd. C3	Regency Rd. B3	Terminus Rd. B1	Windsor St. B3
Centurion Rd. B2	Elmore Rd. D2	King Pl. C3	Newark Pl. D1	Regency Sq. A3	The Lanes C3	York Pl. C1/D1
Chapel St. D3	Foundry St. C2	King's Rd. A3/B4	Newhaven St. D1	Regent Hill B3	Tichborne St. C2	
Cheapside C1	Frederick Gdns. C2	Leopold Rd. B2	North Gdns. B2	Regent St. C2	Tidy St. C1	
Cheltenham Pl. C2	Frederick Pl. C1	Lewes Rd. D1	North Pl. C2	Richmond St. D2	Trafalgar La. C1	
Church St. B2/C2	Frederick St. C2	Lewes St. D1	North Rd. C2	Robert St. C2	Trafalgar St. C1	

Bristol

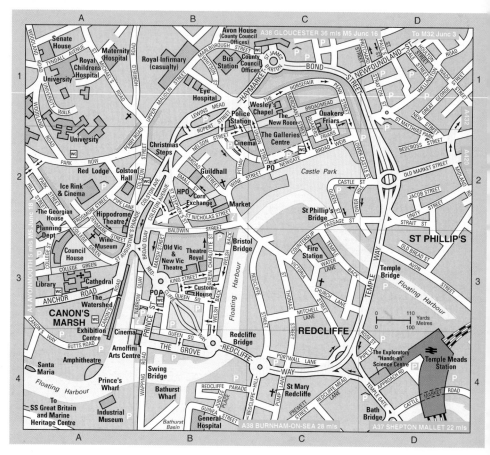

Anchor Rd. A3	Church La. C3	Jacob St. D2	Newgate C2	Quakers Friars C1/C2	St. Matthias Park D1/D2	Tower Hill C2
Approach Rd. D4	College Gn. A3	Jubilee Pl. B4	Old Bread St. D3	Queen Charlotte St. B3	St. Michael's Rd. A1	Tyndall Ave. A1
Avon St. D3	College St. A3	King St. B3	Old Market St. D2	Queen Sq. C3/4	St. Nicholas St. B2	Union St. C2
Baldwin St. B3	Colston Ave. B2	Lewins Mead B1	Park Row A2	Redcliffe Hill C4	St. Paul's St. D1	Unity St. D2
Bond St. C1	Counterslip C3	Lwr Castle St. C2/D2	Park St. A2	Redcliffe Mead La. C4	St. Stephen's St. B2	University Walk A1
Broad Quay B3	Dale St. D1	Marlborough St. B1	Passage St. C2	Redcliffe Pde. B4	St. Thomas St. C3	Upper Maudlin St. B1
Broad St. B2	Denmark St. A2/3	Marsh St. B3	Penn St. C1	Redcliffe St. C3	Small St. B2	Victoria St. C3
Broadmead C1	Frogmore St. A2	Merchant St. C1	Perry Rd. A2	Redcliffe Way B3/C4	Strait St. D2	Wade St. D1
Broad Weir C2	Great George St. D1	Midland Rd. D2	Pipe La. A2	Redcross St. D2	Stratton St. D1	Wapping Rd. B4
Butts Rd. A4	Guinea St. B4	Mitchell La. C3	Pipe La. (Redcliffe) D4	Rose St. D4	Temple Back C3	Wellington Rd. D1
Canon's Rd. A3	Haymarket C1	Narrow Quay B3	Portwall La. C4	Rupert St. B1	Temple Gate D4	Welsh Back B3
Canon's Way A4	Hill St. A2	Nelson St. B2	Prewett St. C4	St. Augustine's Pde.	Temple Way D3	Whitson St. B1
Castle St. C2	Horfield Rd. A1	New St. D1	Pritchard St. D1	A2/A3	The Grove B4	Wine St. B2
Cattle Market Rd. D4	Houlton St. D1	Newfoundland St. D1	Pump La. C4	St. James Barton C1	The Horsefair C1	Woodland Rd. A1

Phone for information

Avoid delays on your journey. Information about roadworks and traffic hold-ups may be obtained by calling the RAC Motorist's Hotline on 0891 500 242.

Calls are charged at 39p per minute cheap rate and 49p per minute at other times.

Cambridge

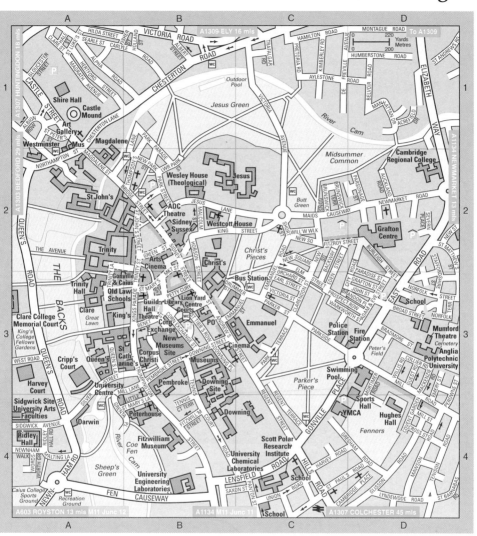

Acrefield Dr. D1
Adam & Eve St. D3
Albert St. B1
Albion Row A1
Alpha Rd. A1
Auckland Rd. D2
Aylestone Rd. C1
Backway C2
Belvoir Rd. D1
Benet St. B3
Botolph La. B3
Bradmore St. D3
Brandon Pl. B3
Bridge St. B2
Broad St. D3
Brunswick Gdns. C2
Brunswick Ter. C2

Burleigh St. D2
Cambridge Pl. C4/D4
Carlyle Rd. A1/B1
Castle St. A1
Chesterton La. A1
Chesterton Rd. B1
City Rd. C3/D2
Clare St. A1
Clarendon St. C3
Collier Rd. D3
Corn Exchange St. B3
Covent Garden D4
Cross St. D4
De Freville Ave. C1
Downing Pl. B3
Downing St. B3
Drummer St. B3/C3

Earl St. C3
East Rd. D2/D3
Eden St. C2/C3
Elizabeth Way D1
Elm St. C2/C3
Emery St. D3
Emmanuel Rd. C2/C3
Emmanuel St. B3/C3
Fen Causeway A4/B4
Fisher St. A1/B1
Fitzroy St. C2/D2
Fitzwilliam St. B4
Glisson Rd. D4
Gloucester St. C1
Gonville Pl. C4
Grafton St. D3
Green St. B2

Grenta Pl. A4
Gresham Rd. D4
Guest Rd. D3
Hale St. A1
Hamilton Rd. C1
Harvey Rd. C4
Hertford St. A1
Hilda St. A1
Hills Rd. C4
Hobson St. B2
Holland St. B1
Humberst.one Rd. D1
Jesus La. C2
John St. D3
Kimberley Rd. C1
King St. B2/C2
Kings Pde. B3

Lensfield Rd. C4
Little St. Mary's La. B4
Lower Park St. B2
Lyndewode Rd. D4
Mackenzie Rd. D3
Magdalene St. A2
Magrath Ave. A1
Maids Causeway C2
Malcolm St. B2
Malting La. A4
Manhattan Dr. D1
Market St. B2/B3
Mawson Rd. D4
Mill La. B3
Mill Rd. D3/D4
Mill St. D4
Montague Rd. D1

Mortimer Rd. D3
New Park St. B2
New Square C2
New St. D2
Newmarket Rd. D2
Newnham Rd. A4
Newnham Walk A4
Norfolk St. D3
Norfolk Ter. D3
Northampton St. A1
Orchard St. C3
Panton St. C4
Paradise St. D3
Park Pde. B1/B2
Park St. B2
Park Ter. C3
Parker St. C3

Parkside C3
Pembroke St. B3
Perowne St. D3/D4
Petty Cury B3
Pretoria Rd. C1
Prospect Row C3
Queen's La. A3
Queen's Rd. A2/A3
Regent St. C3
Regent Ter. C3/C4
Ridley Hall Rd. A4
St. Andrews Rd. D1
St. Andrew's St. B3
St. Barnabas Rd. D4
St. John's St. B2
St. Luke's St. A1
St. Mary's St B3

Cambridge *Index*

continued from page 17

St. Matthew's St. D2
St. Paul's Rd. C4/D4
St. Peter's St. A1
St. Tibb's Row B3
Saxon Rd. B4/C4

Searle St. A1
Severn Pl. D2
Short St. C2
Sidgwick Ave. A4
Sidney St. B2

Silver St. A3/A4
Staffordshire St. D2/D3
Tenison Rd. D4
Tennis Court Rd. B3/B4

Tennis Court Ter. B4
Thompson's La. B1/B2
Trafalgar Rd. C1
Trinity La. A2/A3
Trinity St. B2/B3

Trumpington St. B3/B4
Union Rd. C4
Victoria Ave. C1/C2
Victoria Rd. B1
Victoria St. C3

Warkworth St. C3/D3
West Rd. A3
Willow Walk C2
Willis Rd. D3
Wordsworth Grove A4

Canterbury

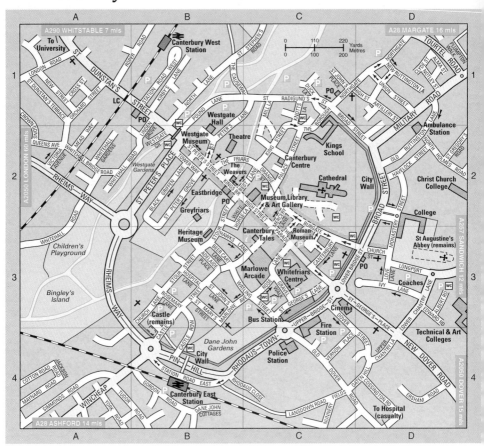

Adelaide Pl. B3
Albert Rd. D3
Alma St. D1
Artillery St. D1
Beer Cart La. B3
Best La. B2/C2
Black Griffin La. B2
Broad St. C1/D2
Burgate C3
Canterbury La. C3
Castle Row B4
Castle St. B3
Church La. B3
Church St. D3
Clyde St. D1
Cossington Rd. D4
Cotton Rd. A4

Cross St. A1
Crown Gdns. A1/2
Dane John Cotts. B4
Dover St. C3/D4
Duck La. C1
Edward Rd. D3
Ersham Rd. D4
Gordon Rd. B4
Gravel Walk C3
Havelock St. D2
Hawks La. B3
High St. C2
High St. D1
Hospital La. B3
Ivy La. D3
Jackson Rd. A4
King St. C2

Kings Bridge B2
Kirby's La. B1
Knotts La. C1
Lansdown Rd. C4
Linden Grove B2
London Rd. A1
Longport D3
Love La. D3
Lwr Bridge St. C3
Lwr Chantry La. D3
Marlowe Ave. B3
Maynard Rd. A4
Mead Way A2
Mercery La. C2
Military Rd. D1
Mill La. C1
Monastery St. D2/D3

New Dover Rd. D4
New Ruttington La. D1
New St. A1
Nth Holmes Rd. D2
North La. B1
Northgate C1/D1
Notley St. D1
Nunnery Fields C4
Oaten Hill D4
Old Dover Rd. C4
Old Ruttington La. D2
Orange St. C2
Orchard St. A1
Palace St. C2
Pin Hill B4
Plumpton Walk D1
Pound La. B1

Queens Ave. A2
Rheims Way A2/A3
Rhodaus Cl. B4/C4
Rhodaus Town C4
Roper Rd. A1/B1
Rose La. C3
Rosemary La. B3
Simmonds Rd. A4
St. Dunstan's St. A1
St. Dunstan's Ter. A1
St. George's La. C3
St. George's Pl. D3
St. Gregory's Rd. D2
St. John's La. B3
St. John's Pl. C1
St. Mary's St. B3
St. Peter's Grove B2

St. Peter's La. B2/C1
St. Peter's Pl. B2
St. Peter's St. B2
St. Radigund's St. C1
St. Stephen's Rd. C1
Station Rd. East B4
Station Rd. West B1
Stour St. B3
The Borough C1
The Causeway B1
The Friars B2
The Parade C3
Tourtel Rd. D1
Tower Way B2
Tudor La. A4/B4
Union St. D1
Upr Bridge St. C3

Upr Chantry La. D4
Vernon Pl. C4
Victoria Ave. A2
Watling St. C3
Westgate Grove B2
White Horse La. B2
Whitehall Br. Rd. A2
Whitehall Gdns. A2
Whitehall Rd. A2/A3
Wincheap A4
York Rd. A4

Cardiff

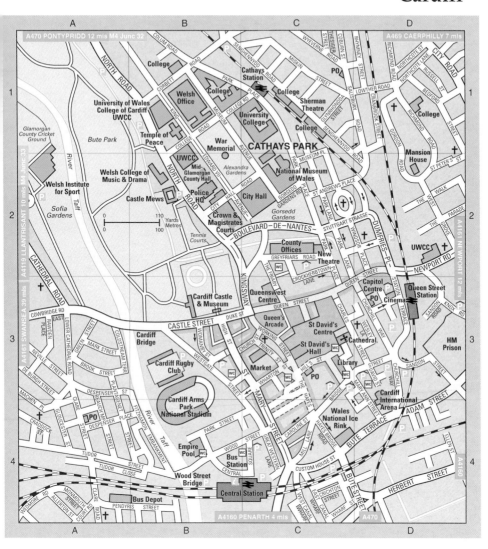

Adam St. D4	City Hall Rd. B2	David St. D3	Hayes Bridge Rd. C4	Museum Pl. C2	St. Andrews Pl. C2	Tudor St. A4
Allerton St. A4	City Rd. D1	De Burgh St. A3	Herbert St. D4	Neville St. A3	St. Mary St. C3/C4	Wedmore Rd. A4
Beauchamp St. A4	Clare Rd. A4	Despenser Pl. A4	High St. B3	Newport Rd. D2	St. Peter's St. D2	Wesley La. D3
Bedford St. D1	Clare St. A4	Despenser St. A3	Hill's St. C3	North Rd. A1/B2	Salisbury Rd. C1/D1	West Canal Wharf C4
Blvd. de Nantes C2	Coburn St. C1	Duke St. B3	King Edw'd VII Ave. B1/B2	Northcote La. D1	Sandon Rd. D3	West Grove D2
Bridge St. C3/D3	Coldstream Ter. A3	Dumfries Pl. D2	Kingsway C3	Northcote St. D1	Sandon St. D3	Westgate St. B3
Brook St. A3	College Rd. B1	East Canal Wharf C4	Knox Rd. D3	Park La. C2	Senghennydd Rd. C1	Wharf St. C4
Bute St. C4/D4	Colum Rd. B1	Ellen St. D4	Lwr Cathedral Rd. A3	Park Pl. B1/C2	Station Ter. D3	Wharton St. C3
Bute Ter. D4	Corbett Rd. B1	Fitzhamon Emb. B4	Lowther Rd. D1	Park St. B4	Stuttgart Strasse C2	Windsor Pl. D2
Caroline St. C4	Court Rd. A4	Gloucester St. A4	Machen Pl. A3/A4	Pendyris St. A4/B4	The Friary C2/C3	Womanby St. B3
Castle St. B3	Cowbridge Rd. East A3	Glynrhondda St. C1	Mark St. A3	Plantagenet St. A3/A4	The Hayes C3	Wood St. B4
Cathedral Rd. A2/A3	Craddock St. A4	Gordon Rd. D1/D2	Mary Ann St. D3/D4	Queen St. C3	The Parade D2	Working St. C3
Central Sq. B4/C4	Cranbrook St. D1	Gorsedd Gdns Rd. C2	Mill La. C4	Rawden Pl. A3	The Walk D2	Wyeverne Rd. C1
Charles St. C3/D3	Crichton St. C4	Great Western La. C4	Miskin St. C1	Rhymney St. D1	Thesiger St. C1	
Church St. C3	Crockherbtown La. C2	Green St. A3	Monmouth St. A4	Richmond Rd. D1	Trinity St. C3	
Churchill Way D3	Custom House St. C4	Greyfriars Rd. C2	Museum Ave. B1/C2	Russell St. D1	Tudor Cl. A4	

Cheltenham

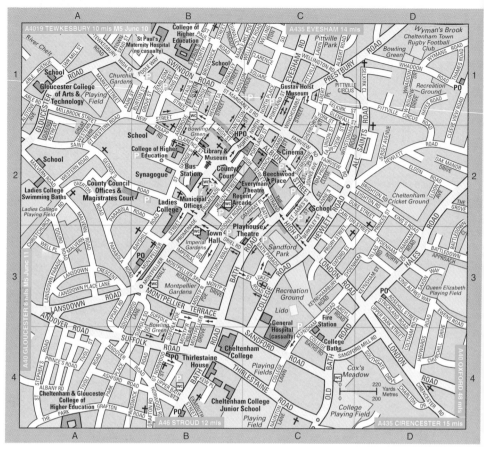

Albany Rd. A4	Charlton Dr. D4	Great Norwood St. B4	London Rd. C3/D4	Overton Rd. A2	Selkirk St. C1	The Grove D2
Albert Pl. C1	Christchurch Rd. A3	Great Western Rd. A2	Lower Mill St. A1	Oxford St. C3	Sherborne Pl. C2	The Park A4
Albert Rd. C1	Churchill Dr. D4	Great Western Ter. A2	Lypiatt Rd. A3	Painswick Rd. B4	Sherborne St. C2	The Strand C2
Albion St. C2	Cirencester Rd. D4	Grove St. B1	Malvern Pl. A3	Parabola Rd. A2/A3	Southgate Dr. D4	Thirlestaine Rd. C4
All Saints Rd. D2	Clarence Sq. C1	Hales Rd. D3	Malvern Rd. A2/A3	Park Pl. A4	Southwood La. A3	Tivoli Rd. A4
Alstone Ave. A1	Clarence St. B2	Hayes Rd. D1	Market St. A1	Park St. A1	St Anne's Rd. C2	Tivoli St. A4
Ambrose St. B2	Cleeve View Rd. D2	Haywards Rd. D4	Marle Hill Pde. B1	Pittville Circus C1	St George's Pl. B2	Tom Price Cl. C2
Andover Rd. A3/A4	College Baths Rd. C4	Henrietta St. B1	Millbrook St. A1	Pittville Circus Rd. D1	St George's St. B1	Townsend St. A1
Argyll Rd. C3	College Lawn C4	Hewlett Rd. C3/D2	Milsom St. B1	Pittville Lawn.C1	St James's St. C2	Union St. C2
Arle Ave. A1	College Rd. C3	High St. A1/C2	Monson Ave. B1	Poole Way B1	St Johns Ave. C2	Upper Bath St. B4
Arle Rd. A1	Coltham Rd. D4	High St. C3	Montpellier Dr. B3	Portland St. C1/C2	St Lukes Rd. C3	Upper Park St. D3
Ashford Rd. A4	Cranham Rd. D3	Imperial Sq. B3	Montpellier Grove B4	Prestbury Rd. C1	St Margaret's Rd. B1	Vittoria Walk B3
Bath Pde. C3	Douro Rd. A3	Jersey Ave. D2	Montpellier Pde. B3	Prince's Rd. A4	St Paul's Rd. B1	Well Pl. A3
Bath Rd. B3/B4	Duke St. C2	Kew Pl. B4	Montpellier Spa Rd. B3	Princes St. D2	St Paul's St. North B1	Wellesley Rd. C1
Bath St. C2	Dunalley Pde. B1	Keynsham Rd. C4	Montpellier St. B3	Priory St. C3	St Paul's St. South B1	Wellington Rd. C1
Battledown Approach D3	Dunalley St. B1	Keynsham St. D3	Montpellier Ter. B3	Promenade B2/B3	St Stephen's Rd. A4	Wellington Sq. C1
Battledown Cl. D3	Eldon Ave. D2	Keynshambury Rd. C3	Montpellier Villas B4	Queens Retreat A2	Strickland Rd. D3	Westbourne Dr. D1
Bayshill Rd. B3	Eldon Rd. D2	King Alfred Way.D3	Montpellier Walk B3	Regent Arcade B2	Suffolk Pde. B4	Western Rd. A3
Bennington St. B2	Evesham Rd. C1	King St. B1	Naunton La. C4	Regent St. B2	Suffolk Rd. B4	Whaddon Dr. D1
Berkeley St. C3	Ewens Rd. D3	King's Rd. D2	New St. B1	Rodney Rd. B2	Suffolk Sq. B3	Whaddon Rd. D1
Brighton Rd. D2	Exmouth St. B4	Knapp Rd. B2	North Pl. C1/C2	Rosehill St. D3	Swindon Rd. B1	Winchcombe St. C1/C2
Brunswick St. B1	Fairview Rd. C2	Lansdown Cres. A3	North St. C2	Saint George's Rd. A2	Sydenham Road North D3	Winstonian St. C2
Burton St. B1	Fairview St. C2	Lansdown Pde. A3	Norwood Rd. B4	Sandford Mill Rd. C4	Sydenham Villas Rd. C3	Wymans Rd. D1
Cambray Pl. C2	Glenfall St. C2	Lansdown Place La. A3	Oak Manor Dr. D2	Sandford Rd. C4	Tewkesbury Rd. A1	York St. C1
Carlton St. C2	Gloucester Rd. A1	Lansdown Rd. A3	Old Bath Rd. C4	Saxon Way D3	Thames Rd. D1	
	Grafton Rd. A4/B4	Leighton Rd. D2	Oriel Rd. B3	Selkirk Cl. D1		

Chester

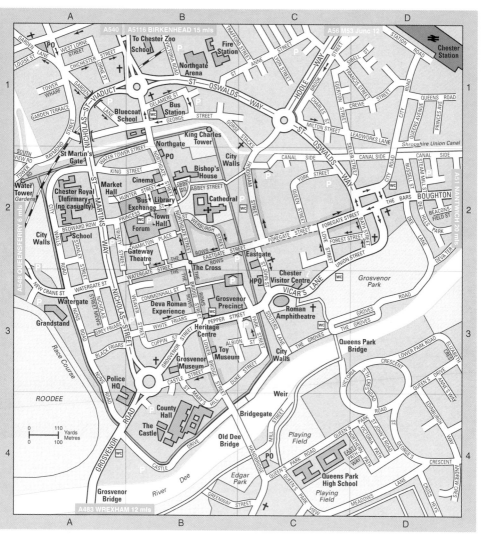

Abbey Sq. B2
Abbey St. B2
Albion St. B3/C3
Andrew Cres. D4
Anne's Way D3
Bath St. D2
Beaconsfield St. D2
Bedward Row A2
Black Friars A3
Boughton D2
Bridge St. B3
Brook St. C1
Canal Side C2/D2
Castle Dr. B4
Castle St. B3
Charles St. C1

Chichester St. A1
City Rd. D1/D2
City Walls Rd. A2
Commonhall St. B3
Cross Heys D4
Cuppin St. B3
Dee Hills Park D2
Dee La. D2
Delamere St. B1
Deva Ter. D2
Duke St. B3/C3
Eastgate St. B2
East Pathway D4
Edinburgh Way D4
Egerton St. C1
Elizabeth Cres. D3

Foregate St. C2
Forest St. C2
Francis St. C1/D1
Frodsham St. C2
Garden La. A1
Garden Ter. A1
George St. B1
Gorse Stacks B1/C1
Greenway St. B4
Grey Friars A3
Grosvenor Rd. A4
Grosvenor St. B3
Groves Rd. D3
Hamilton Pl. B2
Handbridge C4
Hoole Way C1

Hunter St. B2
King St. A2/B2
Leadworks La. D1
Lorne St. A1
Louise St. A1
Love St. C2
Lower Bridge St. B3
Lower Park Rd. D3
Lyon St. C1
Meadow's La. D4
Mill St. C4
Milton St. C1
New Crane St. A3
Nicholas St. A3
Nicholas St. Mews A3
Nicholas St. Viaduct A1

Northern Path D4
Northgate St. B2
Nuns Rd. A3
Pepper St. B3
Princes Ave. D1
Queen St. C2
Queens Ave. D1
Queens Dr. D3
Queens Rd. D1
Queen's Park Rd. C4
Queen's Park View C4
Raymond St. A1/A2
Russell St. D2
St. Anne St. B1/C1
St. George's Cres. D4
St. John St. C2/C3

St. John's Rd. D4
St. Martins Way A2
St. Mary's Hill B3/B4
St. Oswalds Way B1/C2
St Werburgh St. B2
Seller St. C1/D2
Sibell St. D1
Souters La. C3
Sth Crescent Rd. D3
Sth View Rd. A2
Stanley St. A2
Station Rd. D1
Steam Mill St. D2
The Bars D2
The Groves C3
Tower Rd. A2

Tower Wharf A1
Trafford St. B1
Trinity St. A2
Union St. C2/D2
Vicar's La. C3
Victoria Cres. C3/D3
Victoria Path D4
Victoria Rd. B1
Water Tower St. A2
Watergate St. A3/B3
Weaver St. B3
West Lorne St. A1
White Friars B3
York St. C2

21

Chichester

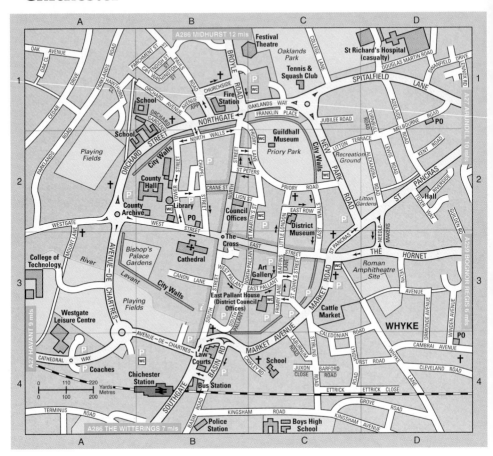

Adelaide Rd. D1	Cathedral Way A4	East Walls C2/C3	Laburnum Rd. C4	North Pallant C3	Priory La. C2	Swanfield Dr. D1
Alexandra Rd. D2	Cavendish St. B1	Ettrick Cl. D4	Lennox Rd. D1	North St. B2	Priory Rd. C2	Terminus Rd. A4
Avenue Approach B1	Cawley Rd. C4	Ettrick Rd. C4	Lewis Rd. D2	North Walls B2	Riverside D2	The Hornet D3
Avenue de Chartres A3/B4	Cedar Dr. A1	Franklin Pl. C1	Lion St. B2	Northgate B1	South Pallant B3	Tower St. B2
Baffins La. C3	Chapel St. B2	Friary La. C3	Little London C3	Oak Ave. A1	South St. B3	Tozer Way D2
Barford Rd. C4	Cleveland Rd. D4	Grove Rd. D4	Litton Ter. C2	Oak Cl. A1	Southgate B4	Turnbull Rd. D1
Basin Rd. B4	College La. C1	Guilden Rd. D2	Lyndhurst Rd. C4/D4	Oaklands Way C1	St. John's St. C3	Velyn Ave. D3
Broyle Rd. B1	Crane St. B2	Hawthorne Cl. A1	Market Ave. C4	Orchard Ave. B1	St. Martin's St. C2	Washington St. B1
Caledonian Rd. C4	Douglas Martin Rd. D1	Jubilee Rd. C1	Market Rd. C3	Orchard Gdns. B1	St. Pancras C3/D2	West Pallant B3
Cambrai Ave. D4	East Pallant C3	Juxon Cl. C4	Melbourne Rd. D1	Orchard St. B2	St. Pauls Rd. B1	West St. B2
Canon La. B3	East Row C2	Kent Rd. D2	Mount La. A3	Ormonde Ave. D3	St. Peters B2	Westgate A2
	East St. C3	Kingsham Ave. C4	Needlemakers D3	Parchment St. B1	Stirling Rd. C4	Whyke La. D4
		Kingsham Rd. B4	New Park Rd. C2	Parklands Rd. A1/A2		Winden Ave. D3

Slow down and save money

Keeping to the speed limits makes economic and environmental sense, and ensures you don't have a brush with the law. The most efficient, fuel-saving speed is between 50 and 60mph. At 70mph, your fuel costs and toxic emissions increase by at least 25%.

Colchester

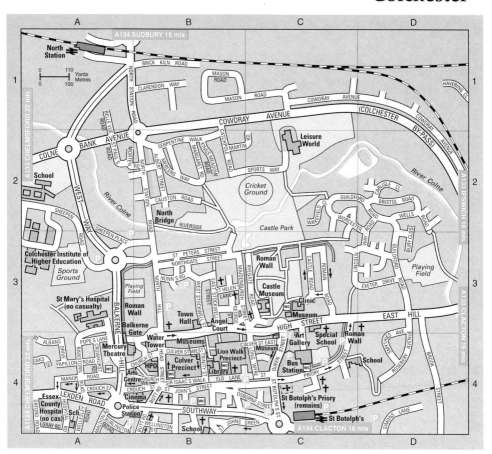

Albert St. B2	Church St. B4	Eld La. B4	Maidenburgh St. B3	Oaks Dr. A4	Sheepen Pl. A3	St Peters St. B3
Balkerne Hill A3/4	Church Walk B4	Exeter Dr. D3	Maldon Rd. A4	Osborne St. C4	Sheepen Rd. A2	Trinity St. B4
Belle Vue Rd. A1	Clarendon Way B1	George St. B3	Manor Rd. A4	Oxford Rd. A4	Simons La. D4	Wakefield Cl. C2
Brick Kiln Rd. B1	Colchester	Gray Rd. A4	Margaret Rd. B2	Papillon Rd. A4	Sir Isaac's Walk B4	Wellesley Rd. A4
Bristol Rd. D2	By.Pass.B1/D1	Guildford Rd. C2/D3	Martin Rd. B2	Pope's La. A4	Smythies Ave. D4	Wellington St. B4
Brook St. D4	Colne Bank Ave. A2	Havering Cl. D1	Mason Rd. B1	Priory St. C4	Southway B4	Wells Rd. D2
Burlington Rd. A4	Cowdray Ave. B1/D1	Head St. B4	Mercers Way B2	Queen St. C4	Sports Way.C2	West Stockwell St. B3
Bury Cl. D3	Crouch St. A4/B4	High St. B4/C3	Morten Rd. A2	Rawstorn Rd. A4	St Albans Dr. A4	West Way.A2
Butt Rd. B4	Crowhurst Rd. A4	Hospital Rd. A4	North Hill B3	Riverside B2	St Botolph's St. C4	Worcester Rd. C2
Carlisle Cl. D2	Culver Street East. C4	Kings Meadow Rd. B2	North Station Rd.	Roman Rd. C3	St Helen's La. B3	
Castle Rd. C3	Culver Street West B4	Lexden Rd. A4	A1/B2	Rosebery Ave. D4	St Johns Gn. B4	
Catchpole Rd. B2	East Hill D3	Lincoln Way.C3	Northgate St. B3	Ryegate Rd. C3	St John's St. B4	
Causton Rd. B2	East Stockwell St. B3	Long Wyre St. C4	Nunn's Rd. B3	Serpentine Walk B2	St Paul's Rd. A2	

Rest easy with RAC Guides

Stopping for the night? There is an RAC accommodation guide to suit every taste and budget.
All publications are available in all good bookshops, or phone for a catalogue on 0800 55 00 55.

Coventry

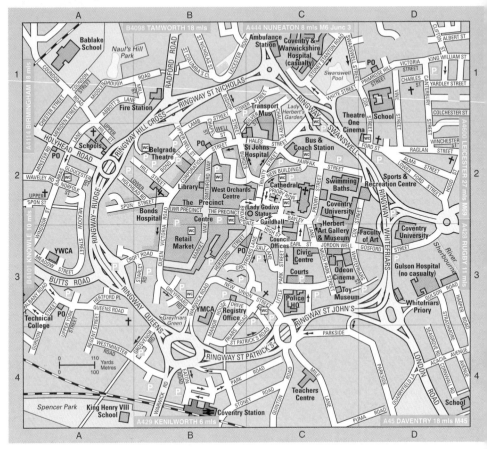

Abbotts La. A1	Clifton St. D1	Grosvenor Rd. B4	Lower Precinct B2	Puma Rd. C4/D4	St. Columba's Cl. B1	Upr Well St. B2
Acacia Ave. D4	Colchester St. D1	Gulson Rd. D3	Manor House Dr. B3	Quarryfield La. D4	St. Nicholas St. B1	Upr York St. A3/A4
Albany Rd. A3	Cornwall Rd. D4	Hales St. C2	Market Way B3	Queen Victoria Rd. B3	St. Patrick's Rd. B4/C4	Victoria St. D1
Albert St. D1	Corporation St. B2	Hertford Pl. A3	Meadow St. A2/A3	Quinton Rd. C4	Salt La. C3	Vine St. D1/D2
Bangor St. B2	Coundon Rd. A1	Hertford St. B3	Meriden St. A1/A2	Radford Rd. B1	Seagrove Rd. D4	Warwick Rd. B3/B4
Barras La. A2	Coundon St. A1	High St. C3	Middleborough Rd. A1	Raglan St. D2	Silver St. C1	Waveley Rd. A2
Bayley La. C2	Cox St. C3	Hill St. B2	Mile La. C4	Regent St. A3/A4	Smithford Way B2	Well St. B2
Bishop St. B1	Croft Rd. A3/B3	Holyhead Rd. A2	Mill St. B1	R'way Hill Cross A2	Spon St. A2/B2	Westminster Rd. A4
Bond St. B2	Earl St. C3	Hood St. D2	Minster Rd. A2	R'way Queens A3/B3	Starley Rd. B3	White St. C1
Broadgate B2	Eaton Rd. B4	Jordan Well C3	Much Park St. C3	R'way Rudge A2/A3	Stoney Rd. B4/C4	Whitefriars St. C3
Burges B2	Fairfax St. C2	King William St. D1	New Buildings C2	R'way St John's C3	Stoney Stanton Rd. C1	Winchester St. D2
Butts Rd. A3	Ford St. D2	Lamb St. B1	New Union St. B3/C3	R'way St Nicholas B1	Strathmore Ave. D3/D4	Windsor St. A2/A3
Canterbury St. D1	Friars Rd. B4	Leicester Row B1	Norfolk St. A2	R'way St Patrick's	Swansell St. C1	Yardley St. D1
Chapel St. B2	Gloucester St. A2	Little Park St. C3	Park Rd. B4/C4	B4/C4	The Precinct B2	
Charles St. D1	Gordon St. A4	London Rd. D4	Parkside C4/D4	R'way Swanswell	Tower St. B1/C1	
Chauntry Pl. C2	Gosford St. D3	Lwr Ford St. D2	Primrose Hill St. D1	C1/C2	Trinity St. C2	
Chester St. A1	Greyfriars La. B3/C3	Lwr Holyhead Rd.	Priory Row C2	R'way Whitefriars	Upr Hill St. A2	
	Greyfriars Rd. B3	A2/B2	Priory St. C2	D2/D3	Upr Spon St. A2	

Don't give car thieves credit

Don't become a victim of crime. Twenty per cent of stolen credit cards and cheque books are taken from cars - always carry them with you.

Croydon

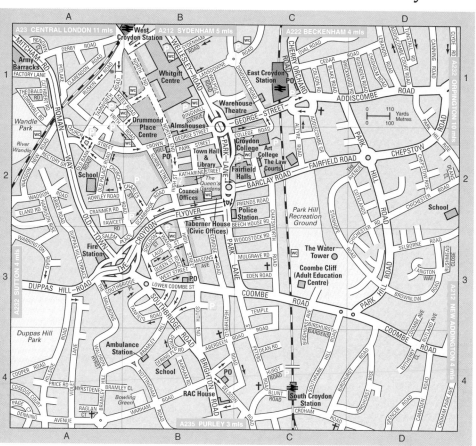

Abbey Rd. A2	Brownlow Rd. D3	Cornwall Rd. A1	Eland Rd. A2
Aberdeen Rd. B4	Campden Rd. D4	Cosedge Court A4	Factory La. A1
Addiscombe Ct. Rd. D1	Canning Rd. D1	Cotelands D2	Fairfield Rd. C2
Addiscombe Grove C2	Cedar Rd. C1/D1	Cranmer Rd. A2	Fawcett Rd. A2
Addiscombe Rd. D1	Charles St. B2	Croham Rd. C4	Friends Rd. C2
Altyre Rd. C2	Chatsworth Rd. C2/C3	Croham Park Ave. D4	Frith Rd. A1/B2
Barclay Rd. C2	Chepstow Rise D2	Crown Hill B2	George St. B2/C1
Barham Rd. B4	Chepstow Rd. D2	Cuthbert St. A1	Harrison Rise A2
Beech House Rd. C2	Cherry Orchard Rd. C1	Dean Rd. C4	Heathfield Rd. B3/B4
Birdhurst Ave. C3/C4	Chichester Rd. D2/D3	Deans Cl. D2	High St. B2/B3
Birdhurst Gdns. C3	Chisholm Rd. D1	Denning Ave. A4	Hillside Rd. A4
Birdhurst Rise D4	Church Rd. A2	Derby Rd. A1	Howley Rd. A2
Birdhurst Rd. C4/D4	Church St. A2/B2	Dering Pl. D4	Hurst Rd. C4
Bisenden Rd. D1	Clarendon Rd. A1	Dering Rd. B4	Hyrstdene A4
Blake Rd. C1	Clyde Rd. D1	Dingwall Ave. B1	Katharine St. B2
Blunt Rd. C4	College Rd. C2	Dingwall Rd. C1	Keely Rd. A1
Bramley Cl. A4	Colson Rd. C1	Duppas Hill Rd. A3	Langton Way D3
Bramley Hill A4/B4	Coombe Ave. D3/D4	Duppas Hill Ter. A3	Lansdowne Rd. B1
Brickwood Rd. C1/D1	Coombe Rd. C3/D4	Eden Rd. C3	Laud St. B3
Brighton Rd. B4	Cooper Rd. A4	Edridge Rd. B3	Lebanon Rd. D1

Lower Coombe St. B3	Renown Cl. A1	Temple Rd. C3
Masons Ave. B3	Roman Way A1/A2	The Avenue D2
Mitcham Rd. A1	Rushmead Cl. D3	The Croydon
Mulgrave Rd. C3	Rutland Ave. D4	Flyover B2/B3
North End B1/B2	Salem Pl. A3/B3	The Waldrons A3
Nottingham Rd. B4	Scarbrook Rd. B2	Theobald Rd. A1
Old Bank Rd. A2	Selborne Rd. D3	Tunstall Rd. D1
Old Palace Rd. A2	Selsdon Rd. B4	Violet La. A4
Old Town A3	Sheldon St. B3	Waddon New Rd. A2
Oval Rd. C1	South End B3	Waddon Rd. A2
Page Court A4	Southbridge Pl. A3	Waldron Hyrst A4
Park Hill Rise D2	Southbridge Rd. B3/B4	Walpole Rd. B1
Park Hill Rd. D2/D3	Southpark Hill Rd. C4	Wandle Rd. B3
Park La. B2/B3	Spencer Rd. D4	Warham Rd. B4
Park St. B2	St. Peters Rd. C4	Warrington Rd. A3
Pitlake A1	Stanhope Rd. C2/D3	Wellesley Rd. B1
Price Rd. A4	Surrey St. B2	West St. B3
Queen St. B3	Sydenham Rd. B1	Witherby Cl. D4
Raglan Court A4	Tamworth Rd. A1	Woodstock Rd. C3
Rectory Grove A2	Tanfield Rd. B3	

Derby

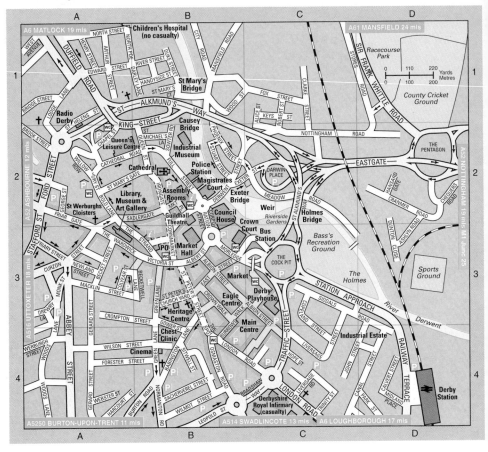

Abbey St. A3/A4
Albert St. B3
Albion St. B3/C3
Alice St. C1
Arthur St. A1
Ashlyn Rd. D3
Babington La. B4
Becket St. A3
Becketwell La. B3
Bold La. A2
Bradshaw Way C4
Bridge St. A1
Brook St. A2
Burrows Walk B3/B4
Burton Rd. A4/B4
Calvert St. D4
Canal St. D4

Cathedral Rd. A2
Chapel St. A2
Chequers Rd. D2
City Rd. B1
Clarke St. C1
Colyear St. A3
Copeland St. A3
Cornmarket. B3
Corporation St. B2
Cranmer Rd. D2
Crompton St. A3
Crown Walk B3
Curzon St. A3
Darley La. B1
Darwin Pl. C2
Derwent St. B2
Drewry La. A3

Duffield Rd. A1
Dunton Cl. D3
East St. B3
Eastgate D2
Edward St. A1
Exeter St. B2
Ford St. A2
Forester St. A4
Fox St. C1
Friar Gate A2
Friary St. A3
Full St. B2
George St. A2
Gerard St. A3/A4
Gower St. B3
Green La. B3/B4
Handyside St. B1

Hansard Gate D2
Harcourt St. A4
Henry St. A1
Hope St. C4
Irongate B2
John St. C4
Jury St. A2
Keys St. C1
King St. A1/B1
Leopold St. B4
Liversage Rd. C4
Liversage St. C4
Lodge La. A1
London Rd. B4/C4
Macklin St. A3
Mansfield Rd. B1
Market Pl. B2

Meadow Rd. C2
Midland Pl. D4
Monk St. A3
Moreledge B3
Newland St. A3
Normanton Rd. B4
North Pde. A1
North St. A1
Nottingham Rd. C2
Osmaston Rd. B4
Park St. D4
Phoenix St. B2
Queen St. B2
Railway Ter. D4
River St. B1
Sacherverel St. B4
Sadlergate B2

Siddals Rd. C3
Sir Frank Whittle Rd. D1
Sitwell St. B4
Sowter Rd. B2
St. Alkmund's Way B1/C2
St. Helens St. A1
St. Mary's Court B1
St. Mary's Gate A2
St. Peter's Church Yd. B3
St. Peter's St. B3
Stafford St. A3
Station Approach C3
Stores Rd. C1/D1
Stuart St. B2
The Cock Pit C3

The Pentagon D2
The Spot B4
The Strand B3
The Wardwick A3
Traffic St. C4
Trinity St. C4
Victoria St. B3
Webster St. A4
Werburgh St. A4
West Ave. A1
Willow Row A2
Wilmot St. B4
Wilson St. A4
Wood St. B1
Woods La. A4

Wise drivers don't drink

Even after just one drink, you are still more likely to be involved in an accident than if you had
stayed clear of alcohol altogether.

Dover

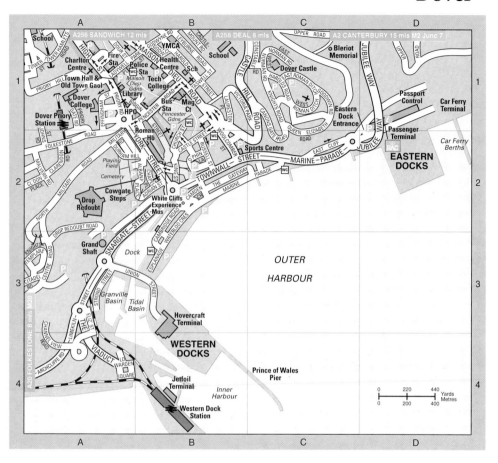

Adrian St. B2	Channel View Rd. A4	East Cliff C2	Harolds Rd. C1	Maison Dieu Rd. B1	Russell St. B2	Upper Rd. C1/D1
Albany Pl. B2	Chapel St. B2	East Norman Rd. C1	High St. A1	Malvern Rd. A2	Snargate St. A3	Victoria Park B1
Archcliffe Rd. A4	Church St. B2	East Roman Ditch C1	Jubilee Way D1/D2	Marine Pde. B2/C2	St Johns Rd. A2	Waterloo Cres. B2/B3
Biggin St. B1	Citadel Rd. A3	Effingham St. A1	King St. B2	Military Rd. A2	Strond St. A3	West Norman Rd. C1
Cambridge Rd. B2/B3	Clarendon Pl. A2	Elizabeth St. A3	Knights Rd. C1	North Military Rd. A2	Taswell St. B1	West Roman Ditch C1
Camden Cres. B2	Clarendon Rd. A2	Esplanade B3	Knights Templars A3	Park St. B1	The Gateway B2	Woolcomber St. B2
Canons Gate Rd. C1	Constable Rd. C1	Folkestone Rd. A2	Ladywell Pl. A1	Pencester Rd. B1	The Viaduct A4	York St. B2
Castle Hill Rd. B1/C1	Dolphin La. B2	Godwyne Cl. B1	Laureston Pl. B1	Priory Gate Rd. A1	Tower Hamlets Rd. A1	
Castle St. B2	Dour St. A1	Godwyne Rd. B1	Leyburne Rd. B1	Priory Hill A1	Tower St. A1	
Castlemount Rd. B1	Drop Redoubt Rd. A2	Goodwin Rd. C1	Limekiln St. A3	Priory Rd. A1	Townwall St. B2	
Centre Rd. A3	Durham Hill A2	Harold St. B1	Lord Warden Sq. A4	Queen Elizabeth Rd. C1	Union St. A3/B3	

Seatbelts save lives

It is the driver's responsibility to ensure that passengers under the age of 14 are wearing seat-belts. Children under the age of 11 should wear an appropriate child restraint. Remember, in the event of an accident at 30mph, a child in a rear seat could be thrown forward with the force equivalent to the weight of a baby elephant.

Dublin

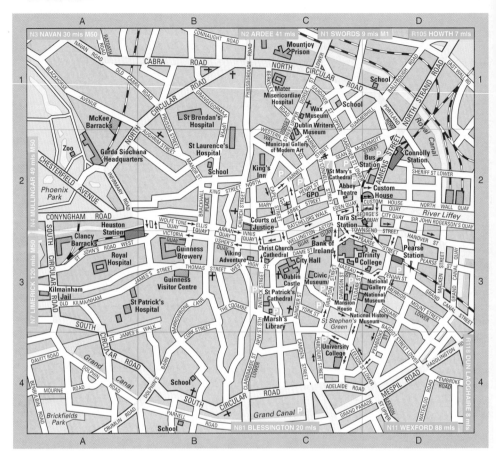

Abbey St. C2
Adelaide Rd. C4
Amiens St. D2
Arran Quay B2
Aston Quay C2
Aughrim St. B2
Aungier St. C3
Baggot St. Lower D4
Ballybough Rd. D1
Batchelor's Walk C2
Benbulin Rd. A4
Berkeley Rd. C1
Blackhorse Ave. A1
Brackenhall Pl. B2
Cabra Rd. B1
Camden St. C4

Capel St. C2
Chesterfield Ave A2
Church St. C2
City Quay D2
Clanbrassil St. Lower B4
Connaught Rd. B1
Conyngham Rd. A2
Cork St. B3
Crumlin Rd. A4
Custom House Quay D2
Dame St. C3
Davitt Rd. A4
Dawson St. C3
Dolphin Rd. A4

Dolphin's Barn B4
Eastwall Rd. D1
Eden Quay C2
Ellis Quay B2
Fenian St. D3
Gardiner St. Upper C1
Gardiner St. Lower C2
Georges Quay D2
Grafton St. C3
Grand Pde. C4
Grand Canal St. D3
Grand Canal Quay D3
Grangegorman Upper B1
Haddlington Rd. D4
Hannover St. D3

Harcourt St. C4
Henry St. C2
High St. C3
Infirmary Rd. A2
Innis Quay B3/C3
James St. B3
Kildare St. C3
King St. North B2
Leeon St. Lower C4/D4
Leeson St Upper D4
Macken St. D3
Manor St. B2
Marowbone La. B3
Mary St. C2
Merrion Sq. D3
Mespil Rd. D4

Mount St. Lower D3
Mourne Rd. A4
Nassau St. C3
Navan Rd. A1
New St. South C3/C4
North Circular Rd. B1/C1
North Wall Quay D2
North Strand Rd. D1
O'Connell St. C2
Old Cabra Rd. A1
Old Kilmainham A3
Parnell Rd. B4
Parnell St. C2
Patrick St. C3
Pearse St. D3

Pembroke St. D4
Pembrole Rd. D4
Phibsborough Rd. B1
Portland Row D1
Prussia St. B1/B2
Ratoath Rd. A1
Sean McDermott St. C2/D2
Sheriff St. Lower D2
Sir John Rogerson's Quay D2
South Circular Rd. A3/A4/B4
St John's Rd. West A3
St James Walk A4
Summerhill C1/D1

The Coombe B3
Thomas St. West B3
Townsend St. C2/D3
Upper Dorset St. C1
Usher's Quay B3
Victoria Quay B3
Waterloo Rd. D4
Wellington Quay C3
Western Sq. C2
Wolfe Tone Quay B2
York St. C3

Dundee

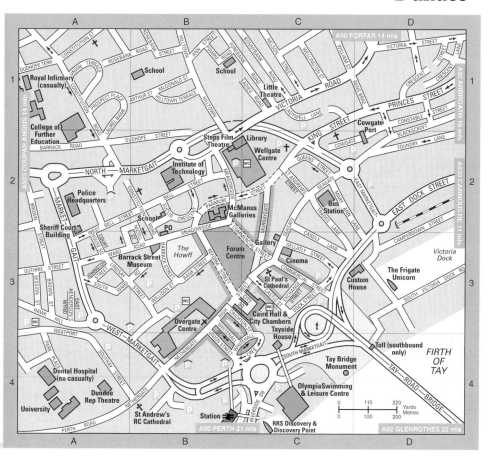

Allan St. D2	City Sq. C3	Dudhope Ter. A1	High St. B3/C3	Nelson St. C1	Rosebank St. B1	Ward Rd. A3/B3
Ann St. B1	Commercial St. C3	Eadies Rd. C1	Hilltown B1	Nethergate B4	Seagate C2	Wellington St. C1
Arthur St. B1	Constable St. D1	East Dock St. D2	Hilltown Ter. B1	Nicoll St. B3	Session St. A3	West Bell St. A2
Bank St. B3	Constitution Rd. A1/B2	East Henderson's	Johnston St. A3	Panmure St. B2	Sth Victoria Dock Rd. D3	West Marketgait A4/B4
Barrack Rd. A2	Constitution St. A1	Wynd A3	King St. C1/C2	Park Pl. A4	South Ward Rd. A3	Westport A3/A4
Barrack St. B3	Court House Sq. A3	East Marketgait D2	Ladywell La. C1	Perth Rd. A4	Southay St. A4	Whitehall Cres. C4
Bell St. B2	Cowgate C2	Euclid Cres. B2	Laurel Bank A1	Powrie Rd. B1	St. Andrews St. C2	Whitehall St. B3/B4
Blackscroft D1/D2	Crescent La. D1	Exchange St. C3	Lindsay St. A3/B3	Princes St. D1	Tay Rd Bridge D4	William St. C1
Bonnybank Rd. C1	Crescent St. D1	Forebank Rd. B1/C1	Market Gait A2/A3	Prospect Pl. A1	Trades La. C2/C3	Willison St. B3
Brown St. A2/A3	Crichton St. B3/C3	Foundry La. D2	Mary Ann La. C2	Queens St. C2	Union St. B4	
Camperdown St. D2/D3	Dens Brae D1	Gellatly St. C3	McDonald St. B1	Reform St. B3	Union Ter. A1	
Candle La. C3	Dock St. C3	Guthrie St A3	Meadowside B2/B3	Riverside Dr. C4	Victoria Rd. C1	
Castle St. C3	Dudhope St. B2	Hawk Hill A3	Murraygate C2	Rosebank Rd. A1/B1	Victoria St. D1	

What to carry in your car

Don't be at a loss if you break down or are involved in an accident. The following items can be easily stored in your vehicle and will prove useful - torch, hazard warning triangle, jump leads, tow rope, first aid kit, and blanket. In winter, always carry warm clothing and a pair of wellington boots.

Edinburgh

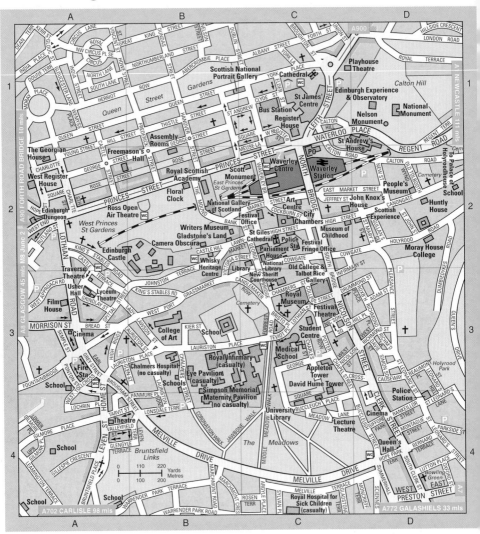

Abercrombie Pl. B1	Canongate D2	Dean Ter. A1	Gladstone Ter. C4	Howe St. A1/B1	Lochrin Pl. A4	Nelson St. B1
Adam St. D3	Castle Hill B2	Doune Ter. A1	Glen St. A3	India Pl. A1	London Rd. D1	New St. D2
Albany St. C1	Castle St. A1/A2	Drummond St. C3/D3	Glengyle Ter. A4	India St. A1	Lonsdale Ter. B4	Nice Sq. C3
Argyle Pl. C4	Castle Ter. A2/A3	Dublin St. B1/C1	Gloucester La. A1	Infirmary St. C3	Lothian Rd. A2/A3	Nicolson St. C3/D3
Bank St. B2	Chalmers St. B3/B4	Dumbiedykes Rd. D2/D3	Gloucester St. A1	Jawbone Walk B4/C4	Lothian St. C3	North Bridge C2
Beaumont Pl. D3	Chambers St. C3	Dundas St. B1	Grassmarket B3	Jeffrey St. C2	Lower Gilmore Pl. A4	North La. A1
Bernard Ter. D4	Chapel St. C3	Earl Grey St. A3	Great King St. B1	Johnston Ter. B3	Lutton Pl. D4	Northumberland St. B1
Bread St. A3	Charles St. C3	East Market St. C2/C3	Grindlay St. A3	Kerr St. A1	Marchmont Cres. B4	Old Tolbooth Wynd D2
Bristo St. C3	Charlotte Sq. A2	Elder St. C1	Gullan's Cl. D2	Kier St. B3	Marchmont Rd. B4	Oxford St. D4
Brougham St. A3/B4	Circus La. A1	Forrest Rd. C3	Hanover St. B1	King's Stables Rd. A2/B3	Market St. C2	Panmure Pl. B4
Broughton St. C1	Circus Pl. A1	Forth St. C1	Herriot Row A1/B1	Lady Lawson St. B3	Meadow La. C4	Parkside St. D4
Bruntsfield Pl. A4	Clerk St. D4	Fountainbridge A3	High Riggs A3	Lauriston Gdns. B3/B4	Melville Dr. B4/C4	Pleasance St. D3
Buccleuch Pl. C4	Clyde St. C1	Frederick St. B1/B2	Hill St. A1	Lauriston Pl. B3	Melville Ter. C4	Ponton St. A3
Buccleuch St. D4	Cockburn St. C2	George Sq. C3	Hillside Cres. D1	Lauriston St. B3	Meuse La. C1/C2	Potter Row C3
Calton Hill C1	Coronation Walk B4	George St. A2/B1	Holyrood Rd. D2	Lawn Market B2	Moncrieff Ter. D4	Princes St. A2/B2
Calton Rd. C2/D2	Cowgate C2	George IV Bridge C2/C3	Home St. A4	Leamington Ter. A4	Montague St. D4	Queen St. A1/B1
Candlemaker Row C3	Cross Causeway D3	Gillespie Cres. A4	Hope Park Ter. D4	Leith St. C1	Moray Pl. A1	Queen's Dr. D3
Canning St. A2/A3	Davie St. D3	Gilmore Pl. A4	Hope St. A2	Leven St. A4	Morrison St. A3	Rankeillor St. D4

Edinburgh *Index*

Regent Rd. D1/D2
Regent Ter. D1
Richmond La. D3
Richmond Pl. D3
Rose St. A2/B2
Rosen Ter. C4
Roxburgh Pl. D3

Royal Circus A1
Royal Ter. D1
Rutland Sq. A2
Rutland St. A2
St. John St. D2
St. Leonard's Hill D3
St. Leonard's La. D4

St.Leonard's St. D3/D4
St. Mary's St. D2
St. Vincent St. A1
Sciennes D4
Semple St. A3
Simon Sq. D3
South Bridge C2/C3

Sth Clerk St. D4
Sth Charlotte St. A2
Sth College St. C3
South La. A1
Spittal St. A3
Summerhall D4
Sylvan Pl. C4

Tarvit St. A4
Teviot Pl. C3
The Mound B2
Thistle St. B1
Union St. C1
Upper Gilmore Pl. A4
Victoria St. B2/B3

Warrender Park Rd. B4
Warrender Park Ter. B4
Waterloo Pl. C1
Waverley Bridge C2
Wemyss Pl. A1
West Approach Rd. A3
West End A2

West Port B3
West Preston St. D4
West Register St. C1
West Tollcross A3
York La. C1
York Pl. C1
Young St. A2

Exeter

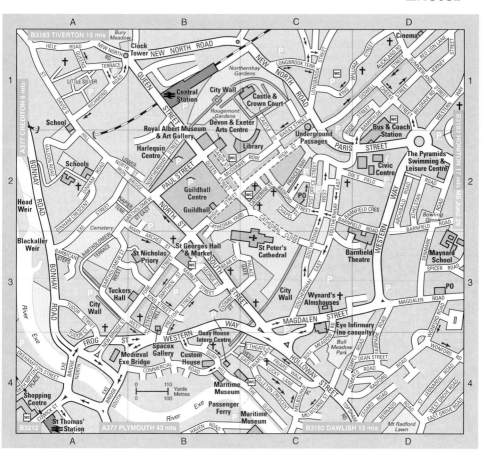

Archibald Rd. D2
Athelstan Rd. D2
Auckland Rd. D1
Bailey St. C2
Bampfylde St. D1
Barbican Steps A3
Barnfield Cres. C2/C2
Barnfield Rd. C2/D2
Bartholomew St. East B2
Bartholomew St. West A3
Bartholomew Ter. A3
Bear St. B3
Bedford St. C2
Belgrave Rd. D1
Bernado Rd. D4
Bonhay Rd. A2/A3

Bude St. C1/D1
Bull Meadow Rd. C4
Castle St. C1/C2
Cathedral Cl. C2/C3
Cathedral Yard B2
Catherine St. C2
Cedars Rd. D4
Chapel St. C2
Cheeke St. D1
Colleton Cres. C4
Commercial Rd. B4
Coombe St. B3
Cowick St. A4
Dean St. D4
Denmark Rd. D2/D3
Dinham Cres. A2

Dinham Rd. A2
Dix's Field C2/D2
East Grove Rd. D4
Exe Bridge North A4
Exe Bridge South A4
Exe St. A2/A3
Fairpark Rd. D3/D4
Fore St. B3
Friars Walk C4
Friars Gate C4
Frog St. A4
Gandy St. B2
George St. B3
Haldon Rd. A2
Haven Rd. B4
Hele Rd. A1

High St. B2/C2
Holloway St. C4
Iron Bridge A2/B2
King St. B3
King William St. C1/D1
Little Silver A1
Longbrook St. C1
Longbrook St. C1
Lower North St. A2
Lucky La. C4
Magdalen Rd. D3
Magdalen St. C3
Market St. B3
Mary Arches St. B2/B3
Melbourne Pl. C4
Melbourne St. C4

Musgrave Row B2/C2
Napier Ter. A2
New Bridge St. A3/A4
New North Rd. B1/C1
North St. B2
Northernhay St. B2
Okehampton Pl. A4
Okehampton St. A4
Palace Gate C3
Paris St. C2/D2
Paul St. B2
Post Office St. C2
Preston St. B3
Princes Way C4
Quay Hill B4
Queen St. B1/B2

Queens Ter. A1
Radford Rd. D4
Red Lion Ln. D1
Richmond Rd. A1
Roberts Rd. C4/D4
St. David's Hill A1/A2
St. Leonards Rd. D4
Sidwell St. D1
South St. B3
Southernhay East
  C2/C3
Southernhay West
  C2/C3
Southgate C4
Spicer Rd. D3
Stepcote Hill B3

Summerland St. D1
Temple Rd. C4/D4
The Quay C4
Topsham Rd. C4
Tudor Court A4
Tudor St. A3
Tudor St. D1
Verney St. D1
West Grove Rd. D4
Western Way B3/B4
Western Way D1/D3
Westgate C4
Wonford Rd. D4

Folkestone

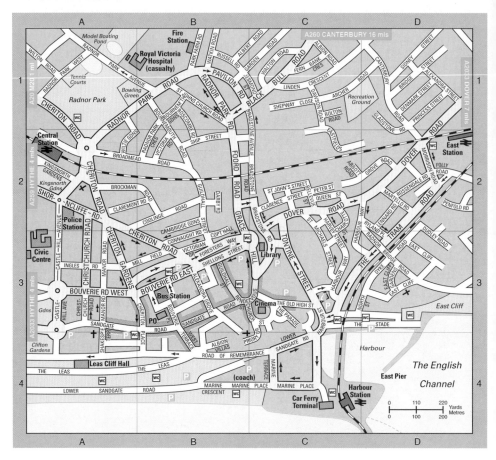

Abbott Rd. C2	Bradstone Ave. C1	Connaught Rd. B3	Gladstone Rd. D1	Marine Pl. B4/C4	Radnor Park Rd. A1/B1	St John's St. C2
Albert Rd. B1	Bradstone Rd. C2	Coolinge Rd. B2	Grace Hill B2	Marine Ter. C4	Rendezvous St. B3	St Michaels St. C3
Albion Rd. C1	Bridge St. D1	Copthall B3	Grove Rd. D2	Martello Rd. D2	Road of	The Leas A4/B4
Albion Villas B4	Broadmead Rd. A2	Darby Rd. B2	Guildhall St. B2/B3	Mill Field B3	Rememberance B4	The Old High St. C3
Alexandra Grove B3	Brockman Rd. A2	Dawson Rd. C1	Harbour St. C3	Morrison Rd. D2	Russell Rd. B1	The Parade C3
Alexandra St. D1	Cambridge Gdns. B2	Denmark St. D1	Harbour Way C3	North Dyke Rd. D3	Ryland Pl. D2	The Stade D3
Archer Rd. C1	Canterbury Rd. D1	Dover Rd. C2/D2	Harvey St. C2	Park Farm Rd. B1	Sandgate Rd. A3/B3	The Tram Rd. C3
Bellevue St. C2	Castle Hill Ave. A3	Dudley Rd. D3	Ingles Rd. A3	Pavillion Rd. B1	Shakespeare Ter. A4	Tontine St. C3
Black Bull Rd. C1	Charlotte St. C2	East Cliff Gdns. D3	Jesmond St. B1	Penfold Rd. D2	Shellons St. B3	Victoria Rd. B2
Bolton Rd. C1	Cheriton Gdns. A3	East Cliff D3	Kingsnorth Gdns. A2	Peter St. C2	Shepway Cl. C1	Victorian Grove.B3
Boscombe Rd. B1	Cheriton Pl. B3	Eastfields C2	Lennard Rd. D2	Princess St. D1	Ship St. B2	Walton Rd. C1
Bournemouth Gdns. B1	Cheriton Rd. A1/B3	Fern Bank Cres. C1	Linden Cres. C1	Priory Grove C4	Shorncliffe Rd. A2	Watkin Rd. B1
Bournemouth Rd. B1	Christchurch Rd. A3	Folly Rd. D2	Lower Sandgate Rd.	Queen St. C2	Sidney St. D1	West Ter. B4
Bouverie Pl.B3	Church St. C3	Foord Rd. B2	A4	Radnor Bridge Rd. D3	St John's Church Rd.	Wiltie Gdns. A2
Bouverie Road East B3	Claremont Rd. A2	Foresters Way B3	Manor Rd. A3	Radnor Park Ave. A1	B1	Wilton Rd. A1
Bouverie Road West A3	Clarence St. C2	Garden Rd. C1	Marine Cres. B4	Radnor Park Cres. B2	St John's St. C2	

Glasgow

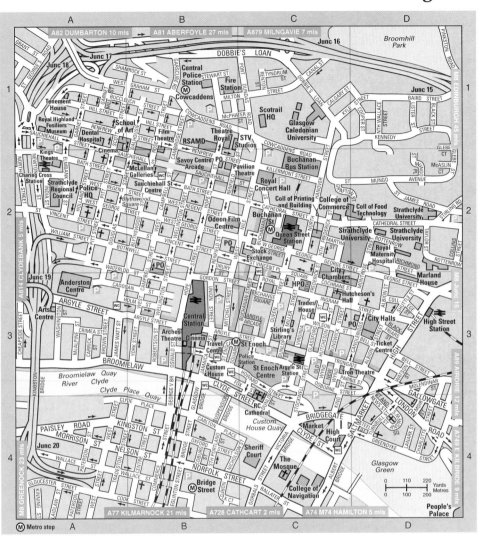

Albert Bridge C4	Cadogan St. A3/B3	Commerce St. B4	Garscube Rd. B1	Hutcheson St. C3	Maxwell St. C3	Osborne St. C3
Albion St. D3	Calgary St. C1	Cook St. A4/B4	George V Bridge B3/B4	India St. A2	Miller St. C3	Oswald St. B3
Argyle Arcade C3	Cambridge St. B1	Cooper St. D1	George Sq. C2	Ingram St. C3/D3	Milton St. B1/C1	Oxford St. B4
Argyle St. A3/B3	Canal St. C1	Cowcaddens Rd. B1/C1	George St. C2/D3	James Watt St. A3	Mitchell St. B3	Paisley Rd. A4
Baird St. D1	Candleriggs D3	Crimea St. A3	Glassford St. C3	Kennedy St. D1	Moir St. D4	Parnie St. C3/D3
Bath St. A2/B2	Carlton Pl. B4	Dalhouse St. B1	Glebe Court D1	King St. C3/C4	Molendinar St. D3	Paterson St. A4
Bell St. D3	Carnoustie St. A4	Dobbie's Loan B1/C1	Glebe St. D2	Kingston Bridge A3	Montrose St. D2/D3	Pinkston Rd. D1
Blackfriars St. D3	Carrick St. A3	Douglas St. A2	Gloucester St. A4	Kingston St. A4/B4	Morrison St. A4	Pitt St. A2
Black St. D1	Cathedral St. C2/D2	Drury St. B2	Gorbals St. C4	Kinning St. A4	Nelson St. A4/B4	Port Dundas Rd. C1
Blythswood St. A2/B2	Centre St. B4	Duke St. D3	Gordon St. B3	Kyle St. C1	New Wynd C3	Queen St. C3
Both Well St. A2	Charlotte St. D4	Dunlop St. C3/C4	Grafton St. C2	Laidlaw St. A4	Newton St. A1/A2	Renfield St. B2
Bridgegate C4	Cheapside St. A3	Eglinton St. B4	Grant St. A1	Lanark St. D4	Nicholson St. B4	Renfrew St. A1/C2
Bridge St. B4	Clyde Pl. B4	Elmbank St. A2	Greendyke St. D4	Lister St. D1	Norfolk Court B4	Renton St. C1
Broomielaw A3/B3	Clyde St. C4	Frederick St. C2/C3	Hill St. A1/B1	London Rd. D4	Norfolk St. B4	Richmond St. D2
Brown St. A3	Coburg St. B4	Fox St. B3/C3	Holland St. A2	McAlpine St. A3	North St. A2	Robertson St. B3
Brunswick St. C3	Cochrane St. C3	Gallowgate D3/D4	Holm St. A3	McAslin Court D2	North Hanover St. C2	Rose St. B1/B2
Buccleuch St. A1/B1	College St. D3	Garnet Hill St. A1	Hope St. B2/B3	McPhater St. B1	North Wallace St. D1	Rottenrow D2
Buchanan St. C2/C3	Collins St. D2	Garnet St. A1	Howard St. B3/C3	Martha St. C2	Old Wynd C3	Royal Exchange Sq. C3

Glasgow *Index*

St. Andrew's Sq. D4
St. Andrew's St. D4
St. Enoch Sq. B3
St. George's Rd. A1
St. James Rd. D2
St. Mungo Ave. D2

St. Mungo Pl. D2
St. Vincent Pl. C2
St. Vincent St. A2/B2
Saltmkt. High St. C4/D3
Sauchiehall St. A1/B2
Scott St. A1

Shamrock St. A1/B1
Shuttle St. D3
South Portland St. B4
Steel St. D4
Stewart St. B1
Stirling Rd. D2

Stockwell St. C3/C4
Taylor St. D2
Tradeston St. A4
Trongate C3
Turnbull St. D4
Tyndrum St. C1

Union St. B3
Victoria Bridge C4
Virginia St. C3
Wallace St. A4
Washington St. A3
Waterloo St. A2/B3

Watson St. D3
Wellington St. B3
West St. A4
West Campbell St. B2/B3
West George St. A2/C2

West Graham St. A1/B1
West Nile St. B2/C2
West Regent St. A2/B2
William St. A2
Wilson St. C3
York St. B3

Gloucester

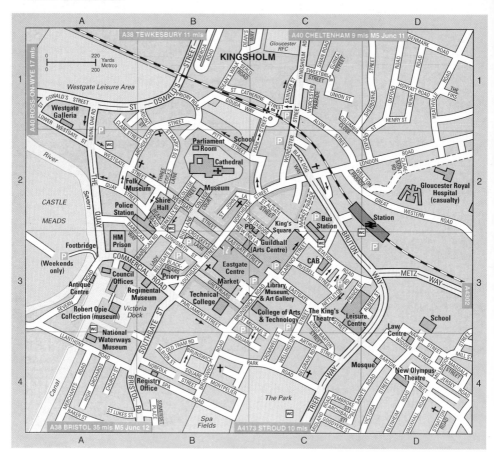

Albert St. D3
Albion St. B4
All Saints Rd. C4/D4
Alvin St. C1/C2
Archdeacon St. B1/B2
Archibald St. C4
Arthur St. C4
Baker St. A4
Barbican Rd. B3
Barbican Way A2/B3
Barton St. D4
Bearland B2
Belgrave Rd. C4
Berkeley St. B2
Black Dog Way C2
Blackfriars. B3
Blenheim Rd. B4

Bristol Rd. A4
Brunswick Rd. B3/B4
Brunswick Sq. B4
Bruton Way C3/D3
Bull La. B2/B3
Church St. A4
Clare St. A1/A2
Claremont Rd. D2
Clarence St. C3
College Court B2
College St. B2
Columbia Cl. C1
Commercial Rd. A3/B3
Cromwell St. C4
Crosskeys La. B3
Dean's Walk B1
Dean's Way B1

Denmark Rd. D1
Eastgate St. B3/C3
Goodyere St. C4
Gouda Way. B1
Great Western Rd. D2
Greyfriars. B3
Guinea St. C1
Heathville Rd. D1
Henry St. D1
Henry St. D1
High Orchards A4
Honyatt Rd. D1
Jersey Rd. D4
King's Sq. C2
Kingsholm Rd. C1
Lady Bellegate St. B3

Llanthony Rd. A4
London Rd. D2
Longsmith St. B3
Lwr Westgate St. A1
Magdala St. D4
Market Pde. C2
Merchants Rd. A4
Mercia Rd. B1
Metz Way D3
Midland Rd. C4
Mill St. D4
Millbrook St. D4
Montpelier B4
Mount St. B1
Napier St. D4
Nettleton Rd. C3
New Inn La. B2/C3

Norfolk St. B4
Northgate St. B2/C2
Old Tram Rd. B4
Oxford Rd. D1
Oxford St. D2
Park Rd. C4
Parkend Rd. C4
Park St. C1/C2
Parliament St. B3
Pembroke St. C4
Pitt St. B2
Prince St. C3
Priory Rd. B1
Quay St. A2
Royal Oak Rd. A1/A2
Russell St. C3
Serlo Rd. B1

Severn Rd. A3
Sherborne St. D1
Skinner St. C1
Somerset Pl. B4
Southgate St. B3
Spa Rd. B4
St. Aldate St. C2
St. Catherine St. B1
St. John's La. B2
St. Lukes St. A4
St. Mary's Sq. B2
St. Michael's Sq. C3
St. Oswald's St. A1/B1
Station Rd. C3
Stratton Rd. D4
Swan Rd. C1
Sweetbriar St. C1

The Firs D1
The Oxbode C2
The Quay A2
Three Cocks La. B2
Trier Way C4
Union St. C1
Vauxhall Rd. D4
Victoria St. D4
Wellington Pde. C2/D2
Wellington St. C4
Westgate St. A2/B2
Widden St. D4
Worcester Pde. C1
Worcester St. C1/C2

Guildford

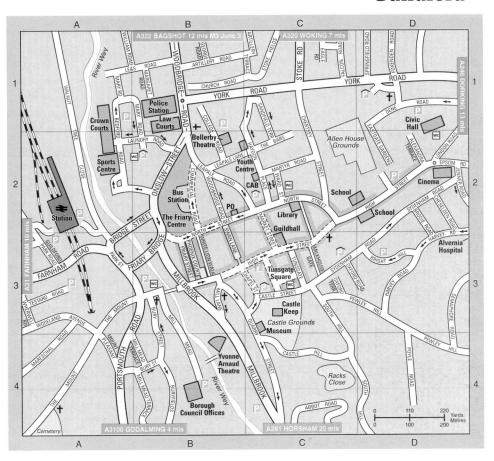

Abbot Rd. C4	Chapel St. C3	Foxenden Rd. D1	Leas Rd. A1	Mount Pleasant A4	Semaphore Rd. D3	Walnut Tree Cl. A1
Alexandra Ter. D2	Chertsey St. C1	Friary Br. B3	London Rd. D2	North St. B2/C2	South Hill C3/D4	Ward St. C2
Artillery Rd. B1	Cheselden Rd. D2	Friary St. B3	Mareschal Rd. A4	Onslow St. B2	Springfield Rd. D1	Wherwell Rd. A3
Artillery Ter. C1	Church Rd. B1	George Rd. B1	Margaret Rd. B1	Oxford Rd. C3	Stoke Fields C1	White Lion Walk B3
Bedford Rd. A1	College Rd. B1	Guildford Park Rd. A3	Market St. C2	Oxford Ter. C3	Stoke Rd. C1	William Rd. A1
Bridge St. A3	Commercial Rd. B2	Harvey Rd. D3	Martyr Rd. C2	Park St. A3	Swan La. B3	Wodeland Ave. A3
Bright Hill D3	Dene Rd. D1	Haydon Pl. C2	Mary Rd. A1/B1	Pewley Hill C3/D4	Sydenham Rd. C3/D2	Woodbridge Rd. B1/B2
Brodie Rd. D2	Eagle Rd. C1	High St. C3/D2	Milkhouse Gate C3	Phoenix Court B3	Testard Rd. A3	York Rd. B1/C1
Bury St. B3/B4	Eastgate Gdns. D2	Jenner Rd. D2	Mill La. B3	Portsmouth Rd. A4	The Bars C2	
Buryfields B4	Epsom Rd. D2	Laundry Rd. B2	Mill Mead B3	Poyle Rd. D4	The Mount A3/A4	
Castle Hill C4	Falcon Rd. C1	Leapale La. B2	Mill Mead Ter. B4	Quarry St. C3	Tunsgate C3	
Castle St. C3	Farnham Rd. A3	Leapale Rd. B2	Millbrook B3/C4	Sandfield Ter. C1	Tunsgate Sq. C3	

Phone for information

Avoid delays on your journey. Information about roadworks and traffic hold-ups may be obtained by calling the RAC Motorist's Hotline on 0891 500 242.

Calls are charged at 39p per minute cheap rate and 49p per minute at other times.

Halifax

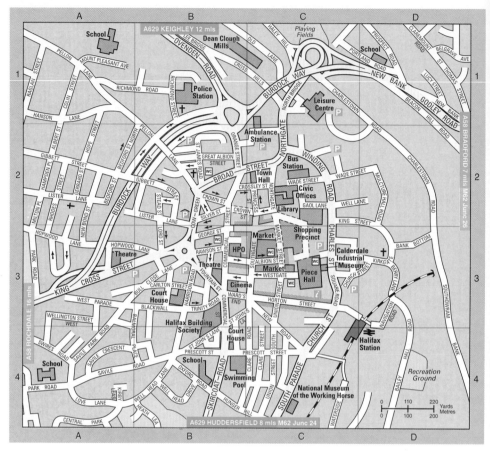

Albert St. A2	Central Park A4	George St. B3	King St. C2	New Rd. C3	Rhodes St. A2	Stead St. B2
Albion St. C3	Charles St. C3	Gerrard St. A2	Kirby Leas A4	North Bridge C1	Richmond Rd. A1	Swires Rd. A4
Bailey Hall Rd. D4	Charlestown Rd. C1/D2	Gibbett St. A2/B2	Kirkgate D3	Northgate C2	Richmond St. B1	Trinity Rd. B3
Balmoral Pl. A3/B4	Church St. C4/D3	Godley Rd. D1	Lee Bridge B1	Old La. C1	Savile Cres. A4	Union St. C3
Bank Bottom D3	Clare Rd. C4	Great Albion St. B2	Lister La. A2/B2	Orange St. B2	Savile Rd. A4	Union St. South C4
Beacon Hill Rd. D1/D2	Clare St. C4	Haley Hill C1	Lord St. B3	Ovenden Rd. B1	Savile Park Rd. A4	Wade St. C2
Bedford St. A2	Claremount Rd. D1	Hampden Pl. A2	Love La. A4	Oxford Rd. B4	Silver St. B2	Ward's End B3
Bedford St North A2	Colin St. A1	Hanson La. A1	Lucy St. D1	Park Rd. A3	Skircoat Rd. B4	Waterside C4
Belgrave Ave. D1	Commercial St. B3	Harrison Rd. B3	Market St. C3	Pellon La. A1/B2	South Pde. C4	Well Head Dr. B4
Berry La. D3	Cow Gn. B2	Heath Lea B4	Milton Pl. A2	Portland Rd. D1	Southgate C3	Well Head La. B4
Blackwall B3	Cross Hills B1/C1	Hope St. A2	Mt. Pleasant Ave. A1	Prescott St. B4/C4	Southowram Bank D3	Well La. C2
Broad St. B2/C2	Crossley St. C2	Hopwood La. A3	Mulcture Hall Rd. D2	Princess St. C2	Square Rd. C3	Wellington St West A3
Bull Close La. B3	Crown St. B2	Horton St. C3	Navigation Rd. D3	Prospect Rd. D1	St. James Rd. B2	West Parade A3
Burdock Way A2/C1	Fountain St. B3	Hunger Hill B4	New Bank D1	Raglan St. A1	St. John's La. B3/B4	Westgate C3
Carlton St. B3	Gaol La. C2	King Cross St. A3	New Bond St. A3	Rawson St. B3	St. Thomas St. D1	Winding Rd. C2

Harrogate

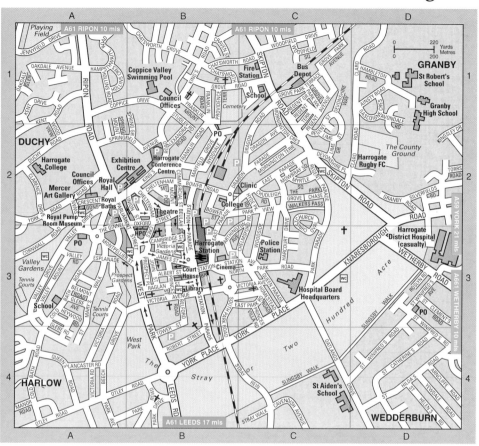

Ainsty Rd. D1
Albert St. B3
Alexandra Rd. B2
Arncliffe Rd. D4
Arthington Ave. B3
Avondale Rd. D1
Beech Grove A3/A4
Belford Rd. B3
Belmont Rd. A3
Beulah St. B2
Bower Rd. B2
Bower St. B2
Cambridge St. B3
Cavendish Ave. C4
Chatsworth Grove B1
Chatsworth Pl. B1
Chatsworth Rd. B1/C1
Chelmsford Rd. C3
Cheltenham Cres. B2/B3
Cheltenham Mount B2
Christchurch Oval C2

Chudleigh Rd. C2
Clarence Dr. A2
Claro Rd. D1/D2
Cold Bath Rd. A3
Commercial St. B2
Coppice Dr. A1/B1
Cornwall Rd. A3
Craven St. B1
Crescent Gdns. A2
Devonshire Pl. C2
Devonshire Way C1
Dragon Ave. C2
Dragon Pde. B2/C2
Dragon Rd. C2
Duchy Rd. A2
East Parade B3/C2
East Park Rd. C3
Esplanade A3
Franklin Mount B1
Franklin Rd. B1/2
Gascoigne Cres. D1

Glebe Ave. A3
Glebe Rd. A4
Granby Rd. D2
Grove Chase C2
Grove Park Ave. C1
Grove Park Ter. C1
Grove Park Walk C1
Grove Rd. B1
Hambleton Rd. D1
Hampsthwaite Rd. A1
Harcourt Dr. C2/C3
Heywood Rd. A3
Hollins Cres. A1
Hollins Rd. A1
Homestead Rd. C3
Hyde Park Rd. C2
James St. B3
Jennyfield Dr. A1
John St. B3
Kent Dr. A1
Kent Rd. A1

King's Rd. B1/B2
Kingsley Dr. D2
Lancaster Rd. A4
Leeds Rd. B4
Lime St. C2
Lime Grove C2
Manor Rd. A4
Mayfield Grove B2
Montpellier St. A3
Mornington Cres. C1/C2
Mornington Ter. C2
Mount Pde. B2
Mowbray Sq. C2
Myrtle Sq. C2
North Park Rd. B3/C3
Nyddvale B2
Oakdale Ave. A1
Oakdale Glen A1
Oatlands Dr. C4
Otley Rd. A4/B4
Oxford St. B2

Park Ave. A4
Park Chase C2
Park Dr. B4
Park Pde. C3
Park Rd. B4
Park View C2
Parliament St. A2/B3
Princes St. B3
Princes Villa Rd. C3
Prospect Pl. B3
Providence Ter. B1
Queen Pde. C3
Queen's Rd. A4
Raglan St. B3
Regent Ave. C1
Regent Grove C1
Regent Pde. C2
Regent St. C2
Regent Ter. C1
Ripon Rd. A1/A2
Robert St. B4

Roslyn Rd. D3
St. Catherine's Rd. D4
St. Clement's Rd. D3
St. Helen's Rd. D4
St. Hilda's Rd. D4
St. Mary's Walk A3
St. Winifred's Ave. D3
St. Winifred's Rd. D3/D4
Silverfields Rd. D2
Skipton Rd. C1/D2
Slingsby Walk C4/D3
South Park Rd. B3/B4
Spring Mount A1/A2
Springfield Ave. A2/B2
Station Ave. B3
Station Bridge B3
Station Pde. B2/B3
Stray Walk C4
Stray Rein C4
Swan Rd. A2
The Ginnel A3

The Grove C2
Torrs Rd. D2
Tower St. B4
Union St. B2
Valley Dr. A3
Valley Mount A3
Valley Rd. A3
Victoria Ave. B3
Victoria Rd. A3/A4
Walkers Pass. C2
West Park B3/B4
Wetherby Rd. D3
Wood View A2
Woodfield Dr. C1
Woodside C3
Yewdale Rd. D4
York Pl. B4/C3
York Rd. A2

Harwich

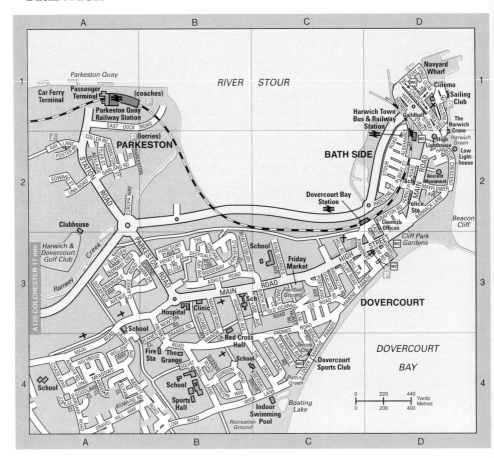

Abbott Rd. A4	Clarkes Rd. A3	Fronks Rd. B4/C3	Highfield Ave. B3	Low Rd. B4	Pelham Cl. A4	The Quay D1
Adelaide St. A2	Cliff Rd. C3	Fryatt Ave. B3	Hill Rd. C3	Lower Marine Pde. C4	Portland Ave. C3	The Ridgeway B3
Ainger Rd. A4	Coller Rd. A2	Garland Rd. A2	Holyrood A4	Main Rd. A4/B3, D2	Pound Farm Dr. B3	The Vineway B3
Albemarle St. D2	Deanes Cl. B4	George St. D1	Ingestre St. D2	Manor La. B4	Queens Rd. B4	Tyler St. A2
Albert St. D2	Deepdale Rd. B3	Goodlake Cl. A4	Jubilee Cl. A4	Manor Rd. B3	Ray Ave. B3	Una Rd. A2
Arderne Cl. A4	Dockfield Ave. A3	Gordon Rd. B4	Kilmaine Rd. A4	Maple Cl. C3	Ray La. A2	Warham Rd. A4
Ashley Rd. B3	East Dock Rd. A1	Gordon Way B4	King Georges Ave. C3	Marine Pde. C3	Seafield Rd. C4	Wellington Rd. D1
Barrack La. D2	East St. D2	Grafton Rd. D2	Kings Quay St. D1	Mayflower Ave. D2	Shaftesbury Ave. B3	West St. D1
Bay Rd. D3	Edward St. A2	Grange Rd. B3	Kingsway C3	Mill La. C3	Squat La. B4	Wick La. B4/C4
Beach Rd. C4	Elizabeth Rd. B3	Gravel Hill Way A4	Kreswell Grove C4	Newton Rd. B3	St. Michaels Rd. C4	Willow Way A4
Birch Ave. C3	Elmhurst Rd. C3	Hall La. B4	Larksfield Cres. B3	Norway Cres. A3	Station Rd. A2	
Briardale Ave. A3	Europa Way A2	Hamilton St. A2	Laurel Ave. A4	Oakland Rd. C3	Stour Rd. D2	
Brooklyn Rd. C3	Fernlea Rd. D2	Harbour Cres. D2	Lee Rd. C3	Old Vicarage Rd. C3	Sweden Cl. A3	
Chase La. A4	Foster Rd. A2	Harcourt Ave. B3	Lime Ave. C3	Orwell Rd. D3	The Close B3	
Church St. D1	Fronks Ave. C4	High St. C3/D3	Long Meadows A4	Parkeston Rd. A2/B3	The Drive C4	

Huddersfield

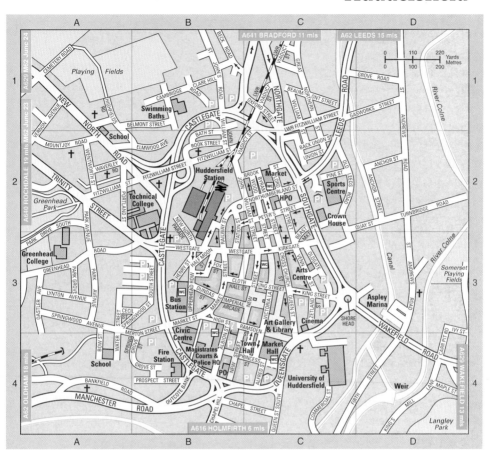

Albion St. B4	Castlegate B1/4	Great Northern St. C1	Lord St. C2	Old Leeds Rd. C2	Railway St. B3	Union St. C2
Alfred St. C4	Cecil St. A3	Greenhead Rd. A3	Lower Fitzwilliam St.	Oldgate C3	Ramsden St. C3	Upperhead Row.B3
Anchor St. D2	Cemetery Rd. A1	Grove Rd. D1	C1	Outcote Bank B4	Rook St. B2	Venn St. C3
Back Union St. C2	Chapel Hill B4	Grove St. B4	Lower Viaduct St. C1	Oxford St. C1	Shore Head C3	Vernon Ave. A1
Bankfield Rd. A4	Chapel St. B4	Half Moon St. B3	Lynton Ave. A3	Park Ave. A2/3	South St. B3	Viaduct St. B2
Bath St. B2	Clare Hil B1	Henry St. B3	Manchester Rd. A4	Park Drive South A3	Southgate C2	Victoria La. C3
Beast Market C3	Cloth Hall St. B3	Highfields Rd. A1	Maple St. D4	Park Grove A3	Spring Grove St. A4	Wakefield Rd. D3
Beaumont St. C1	Commercial St. C4	High St. B3	Market St. B3	Pine St. C2	Springwood Ave. A3	Water St. A4
Beck Rd. B1	Cross Church St. C3	Imperial Arcade B3	Merton St. B3	Portland St. A2	Springwood St. A3	Waverley Rd. A2
Belmont St. B1	Dundas St. B3	Ivy St. D4	Mountjoy Rd. A2	Princess St. C4	St Andrews Rd. D1/3	Wentworth St. A2
Bow St. A4	Elmwood Ave. B2	John William St. B2/C2	New North Pde. B2	Prospect St. B4	St John's Rd. B1	Westgate B3
Brook St. C2	Firth St. C4	King St. C3	New North Rd. A1	Quay St. D2	St Peter's St. C2	William St. C1
Byram St. C2	Fitzwilliam St. A2/B2	King's Mill La. D4	New St. B4/C3	Queen St. C3	Station St. B3	Wood St. C2
Cambridge Rd. B1	Fox St. B3	Kirkgate C3	Northumberland St. C2	Queen Street South C4	Trinity St. A2	Zetland St. C3
Carr Pit Rd. D4	Gasworks St. D1	Leeds Rd. C1	Oastler Ave. A3	Queensgate C4	Turnbridge Rd. D2	

Hull

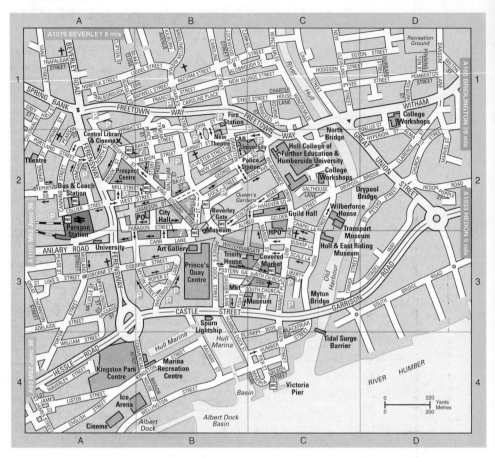

Adelaide St. A3	Charles St. B1	Francis St. B1	John St. B1	Nelson St. C4	Queen St. C4	Sykes St. B1
Albion St. B2	Charter House La. C1	Freetown Way A1/C1	Kilburn Ave. B1	New Cleveland St. C1	Railway St. B4	Tower St. C3
Aldbrough St. B1	Church St. D2	Garrison Rd. C3/D3	King Edward St. B2	New George St. B1	Raywell St. B1	Trafalgar St. A1
Alfred Gelder St. C2	Citadel Way D3	George St. B2	King St. C3	New Garden St. B2	Reform St. B1	Tynem St. B2
Alma St. D2	Clarence St. D2	Great Passage St. A3	Kingston St. A4	Norfolk St. A1	Roper St. B3	Upper Union St. A3
Anlaby Rd. A3	Clifton St. A1	Great Thornton St. A3	Liberty La. C3	North Church Side C3	Russell St. A1	Vane St. A1
Baker St. B2	Coelus St. D1	Great Union St. D2	Liddel St. B1	North St. A2	Salthouse La. C2	Waltham St. B2
Beverley Rd. A1	Collier St. A2	Grey St. A1	Lime St. C1	Osborne St. A3/B3	Saville St. B2	Waterhouse La. B3
Bishop La. C3	Colonial St. A2	Grimston St. B2	Lister St. A4	Paragon St. B2	Scale La. C3	Waverley St. A4
Blackfriar Gate C3	Commercial Rd. B4	Guildhall Rd. B2	Lockwood St. B1	Pearson St. A2	Scott St. B1	Wellington St. B4
Blake Cl. A1	Dagger La. B3	Hall St. A1	Lombard St. A2	Pease St. A3	Silvester St. B2	West St. A2
Blanket Row C4	Dansom La. D1	Hanover Sq. C2	Low Gate C3	Pemberton St. D1	South Bridge Rd. D3	Whitefriargate B3
Bourne St. C1	Davis St. B2	Hedon Rd. D2	Manor House St. B4	Pennington St. D1	South Church Side C3	Wilberforce Dr. C2
Bridlington Ave. B1	Dock Ave. C2	Hessle Rd. A4	Manor St. C3	Percy St. B2	Spring Bank A1	William St. A4
Brook St. A2	Dock St. B2	High St. C3	Market Pl. C3	Pier St. C4	Spring St. A2	Wilton St. D1
Canning St. A2	Drypool Bridge C2	Hodgson St. C1	Marlborough Ter. A1	Popple St. D2	Spyvee St. C1	Wincolmlee C1
Caroline Pl. B1	Durban St. D1	Holborn St. D1	Marvel St. D2	Porter St. A4	St. James Sq. A4	Witham D1
Caroline St. B1	Egton St. C1	Humber Dock St. B3	Melville St. A3	Portland St. A2	St. James St. A4	Wright St. A1
Carr La. B3	English St. A4	Humber St. C4	Midland St. A3	Postern Gate B3	St. Luke's St. A3	
Carr St. B1	Ferensway A2/A3	Hyperion St. D2	Mill St. A3	Prince's Dock St. B3	St. Peters St. C2	
Castle St. B3	Finkle St. C3	Jameson St. B2	Minerva Ter. C4	Princess St. C1	Stephens Sq. A2	
Chapel La. C2	Fish St. B3	Jarratt St. B2	Myton St. B3	Prospect St. A2	Story St. B2	

Ipswich

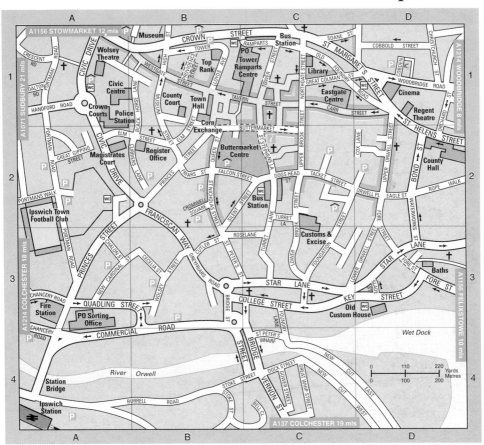

Bell Cl. C4	Cobbold St. D1	Dogs Head St. C2	Greyfriars Rd. B3	Old Foundry St. C1	Slade St. D3	Tower Ramparts B/C1
Black Horse La. B1	College St. C3	Eagle St. D2	Handford Rd. A1	Orchard St. D1	Soane St. C1	Tower St. C1
Bond St. D2	Cobden Pl. D1	Elm St. A2/B2	High St. B1	Orwell Pl. D2	St Helens St. D2	Turret La. C2/3
Bridge St. B3/C4	Commercial Rd. A4	Falcon St. B2	Key St. C3	Portman Rd. A1/3	St Margaret's St. C1	Upper Brook St. C2
Burrell Rd. B4	Cox La. D2	Fore St. D2/D3	Lloyds Ave. B1	Portmans Walk A2	St Nicholas St. B2	Upper Orwell St. D2
Buttermarket C2	Crescent Rd. A1	Foundation St. C3	Lower Brook St. C3	Princes St. A3/B2	St Peter's St. B3	Vernon St. C4
Carr St. C1	Cromwell Sq. B2	Foundry La. C3	Lower Orwell St. D3	Providence St. B1	St Peter's Wharf C4	Waterworks St. D2
Cecelia St. B3	Crown St. B1	Franciscan Way B2	Museum St. B1	Quadling St. A3	St Stephens La. C2	Westgate St. B1
Chalon St. A3	Curriers La. B2	Friars St. B2	New Cardinal St. A3	Queen St. B2	Star La. C3/D3	Wolsey St. B3
Chancery Rd. A3/A4	Cutler St. B3	Great Colman St. C1	New Cut East C4	Rope Walk D2	Stoke St. B4	Woodbridge Rd. D1
Christchurch St. D1	Dalton Rd. A1	Great Gipping St. A2	New Cut West C4	Rose La. B3	Tacket St. C2	
Civic Dr. A1/A2	Dock St. C4	Great Whip St. C4	Northgate St. C1	Silent St. B2	Tavern St. C1	

Slow down and save money

Keeping to the speed limits makes economic and environmental sense, and ensures you don't have a brush with the law. The most efficient, fuel-saving speed is between 50 and 60mph. At 70mph, your fuel costs and toxic emissions increase by at least 25%.

Leeds

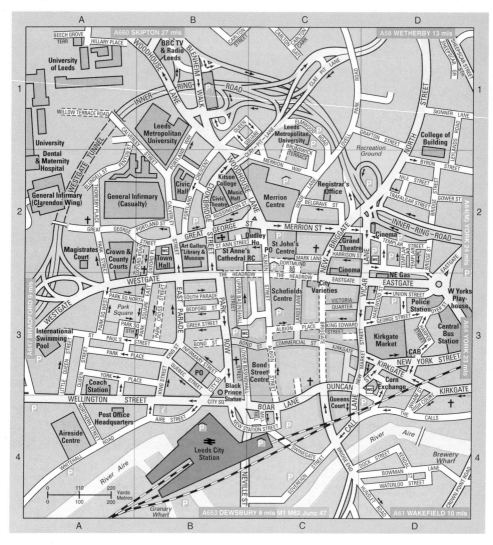

Aire St. B4
Albion Pl. C3
Albion St. C2/C3
Bedford St. B3
Beech Grove Ter. A1
Belgrave St. C2
Blenheim Walk B1
Blundell St. A2
Boar La. C4
Bond St. B3
Bowman La. D4
Bridge End C4
Bridge St. D2
Briggate C3
Brunswick Ter. C1
Byron St. D2
Call La. C4

Calverley St. A1/B2
Carlton Carr C1
Carlton Gate C1
Carlton St. B1
City Sq. B3/B4
Clay Pit La. B2/C1
Cockbridge St. B2
Commercial St. C3
Crown Point Rd. D4
Dock St. D4
Dortmund Sq. C2
Duncan St. C3/D3
Dyer St. D3
East Pde. B3
Eastgate C3/D2
Elmwood Rd. C1
Fenton St. A2

George St. D3
Grafton St. D1
Gt George St. A2/B2
Greek St. B3
Harewood St. D3
Harper St. D3
Harrison St. C2
High Court D4
Hillary Pl. A1
Hunslet Rd. D4
Infirmary St. B3
Inner Ring Rd. B1/D2
Kendal St. D4
King St. B3
King Edward St. C3
Kirkgate C3/D3
Lands La. C3

Leylands Rd. D1/D2
Little Queen St. A3
Lovell Park Rd. C1
Lower Basinghall St. B3
Mark La. C2
Merrion St. C2
Merrion Way C2
Mill Hill C4
Neville St. B4
New Market St. C3/D3
New Station St. B4/C4
New York St. D3
Nile St. D2
North St. D1/D2
Northern St. A4
Oxford Pl. B2

Oxford Row B2
Park Cross St. B3
Park Pl. A3/B3
Park Row B3
Park Sq. East B3
Park Sq. North A3
Park Sq. South A3
Park Sq. West A3
Park St. A2
Portland Cres. B2
Portland St. B2
Portland Way B1/B2
Quebec St. B3
Queen Sq. B1
Queen St. A3
Rossington St. B2
St Ann St. B2

St Pauls St. A3/B3
Sheepscar Grove D1
Sheepscar St. South D1
Skinner La. D1
South Pde. B3
Sovereign St. C4
Swinegate C4
Templar La. D2
Templar Pl. D2
Templar St. D2
The Calls D4
The Headrow B3/C3
Thoresby Pl. A2
Trafalgar St. D2
Union St. D3
Upr Basinghall St. B3
Vicar La. D2/D3

Victoria Quarter C3
Wade La. C2
Waterloo St. D4
Wellington St. A4
Westgate A3/B3
Westgate Tunnel A2
Wharf St. D4
Whitehall Rd. A4
Willow Ter. Rd. A1
Woodhouse La. B1/B2
York Pl. A3

Leicester

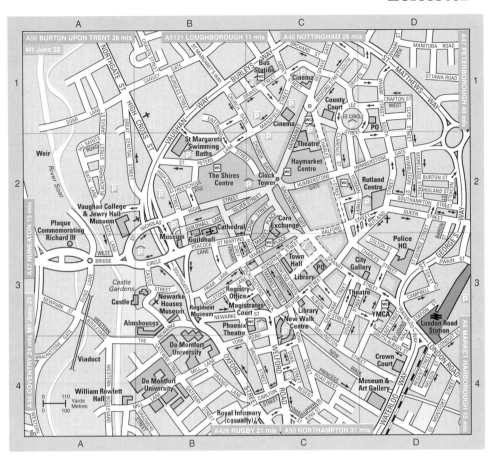

Abbey St. C1
Albion St. C3
All Saints Rd. A2
Baron St. D2
Bath La. A2/A3
Bedford St South C1
Belgrave Gate C1
Belvoir St. C3
Blackfriars St. A2
Bowling Gn St. C3
Braunstone Gate A4
Brown St. C4
Burgess St. B1
Burleys Way B1
Burton St. D2
Campbell St. D3
Cank St. C2

Carlton St. C4
Castle St. B3
Charles St. C2/D3
Chatham St. C3
Church Gate B1/C2
Clarence St. C2
Clyde St. D1
Colton St. D3
Conduit St. D4
Craven St. B1
Crafton St. West D1
De Montfort St. D4
Dover St. B3
Dryden St. C1
Duke St. C4
Duns La. A3
East St. D3

Eastbond St. B1
Fox St. D3
Freeschool La. B2
Friar La. B3
Gallowtree Gate C2
Gateway St. B4
Granby St. C3
Grange La. B4
Grasmere St. B4
Gravel St. C1
Great Central St. A1/A2
Greyfriars B3
Guildhall La. B2
Halford St. C2
Haymarket C2
High Cross St. B1/B2
High St. B2

Horsefair St. C3
Hotel St. C3
Humberstone Gate C2/D2
Jarvis St. A1
King St. C4
Lee St. C1
London Rd. D4
Manitoba Rd. D1
Mansfield St. C1
Market Pl. C2
Market Pl. C3
Market St. C3
Midland St. D2
Mill La. B4
Millstone La. B3
Moreledge St. D2

Nelson St. D4
New Walk C4
Newarke St. B3
Newpark St. A3
Nichols St. D2
Northgate St. A1
Orchard St. C1
Ottawa Rd. D1
Oxford St. B4
Peacock La. B3
Pocklingtons Walk C3
Princess Rd. West C4
Queen St. D2
Regent Rd. C4
Regent St. D4
Rutland St. D2
Sanvey Gate B1

Silver St. B2
Soar La. A1
South Albion St. D4
Southampton St. D2
Southgates B3
St. George St. D3
St. George's Way D3
St. Johns Walk D3
St. Margaret's Way B1
St. Martins B3
St. Mathews Way D1
St. Nicholas Circle B2/B3
St. Peters La. B2
Station St. D3
Swain St. D3
The Newarke B4

Tower St. C4
Upper King St. C4
Vaughan Way B1
Waterloo Way D3/D4
Welford Rd. C4
Wellington St. C4
West Bridge A3
Western Blvd. A3/A4
Western Rd. A4
Wharf St. North D1
Wharf St. South D1
Wimbledon St. D2
Yeoman St. C2
York Rd. B4

Liverpool

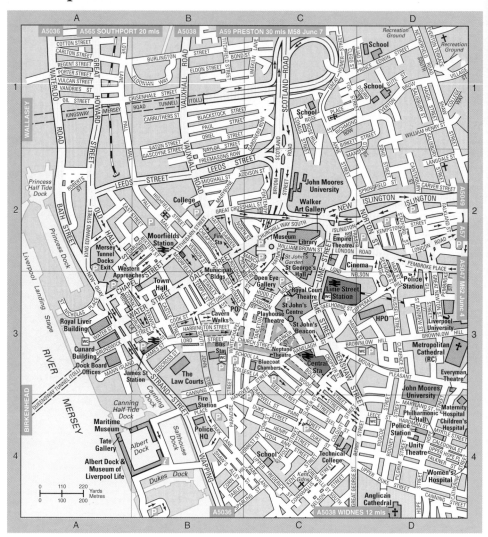

Addison St. B2/C2	Caledonia St. D4	Clarence St. D3	Dale St. B3	Fleet St. C3/C4	Gt. Howard St. A1	Islington C2/D2
Bath St. A2	Canning Pl. B3	Clegg St. C1	Dawson St. C3	Fontenoy St. C2	Gt. Newton St. D3	James St. B3
Berry St. C4	Canning St. D4	College La. B3	Douro St. D1	Formby St. A1	Haigh St. D1	Kempston St. D2
Bevington St. B1	Canterbury St. D2	College Way D1	Drury La. B3	Forrest St. C4	Hanover St. B3/C3	Kent St. C4
Birkett St. C1	Carlton St. A1	Colquitt St. C4	Duke St. C4	Fox St. C1	Hardman St. D4	King Edward St. A2
Bixteth St. B2	Carruthers St. B1	Comus St. C1	Dundee St. A2	Fraser St. C2	Harrington St. B3	Kingsway A1
Blackstock St. B1	Carver St. D2	Cook St. B3	East St. A2	Freemasons Row B2	Hart St. D2	Langdale St. D2
Bond St. B1	Castle St. B3	Copperas Hill C3/D3	Eaton St. B1	Gascoyne St. B2	Hatton Garden B2	Leece St. D4
Bold St. C3	Catherine St. D4	Corn Hill B4	Edmund St. A2/B2	Gill St. D3	Hawke St. C3	Leeds St. A2/B2
Brownlow Hill D3	Chapel St. A3/B2	Cornwallis St. C4	Eldon St. B1	Gradwell St. C3/C4	Haymarket C2	Lime St. C2/C3
Brunswick St. A3/B3	Cheapside B2	Cotton St. A1	Everton Ter. D1	Grenville St. South C4	Henry St. C4	Limekiln Lane C1
Bryom St. C2	Chisenhale St. B1	Covent Garden A3	Falkland St. D2	Gt. Crosshall St. B2/C2	Highfield St. B2	London Rd. C2/D2
Burlington St. B1	Church St. C3	Cropper St. C3	Falkner St. D4	Gt. George St. C4	Hope St. D4	Lord St. B3
Bute St. D1	Churchill Way Sth. C2	Crosshall B2	Fenwick St. B3	Gt. Homer St. C1	Iliad St. C1	Lord Nelson St. C2/D3

44

Liverpool *Index*

Love La. A1
Lydia Ann St. C4
Manchester St. C2
Mann Island A3
Mansfield St. C2/D1
Marybone B2
Maryland St. D4
Midghall St. B2
Moorfields B2
Mount Pleasant D3
Myrtle St. D4
Naylor St. B1/2
Nelson St. C4

Netherfield Rd. South D1
New Islington C2/D2
Newquay A2/A3
North St. B2
Oil St. A1
Old Hall St. A2
Oriel St. B1
Pall Mall A1/B2
Paradise St. B3/B4
Park La. B4/C4
Parker St. C3
Parr St. C4

Paul St. B1
Pembroke Pl. D2/D3
Pilgrim St. D4
Porter St. A1
Preston St. B2
Prince Edwin St. C1/D1
Queensway Tunnel
Ranelagh St. C3
Redcross St. B3
Renshaw St. C3
Richmond Row C1
Roberts St. A2

Rodney St. D4
Roe St. C3
Roscoe St. D4
Rose Hill C1
Rose Pl. C1
Russell St. D3
St. Andrew St. D3
St. Anne St. C1/C2
St. Hood St. C3
St. Nicholas Pl. A3
Salisbury St. D1
School La. B3/C3
Scotland Rd. C1/C2

Seel St. C3/C4
Seymour St. D2/D3
Shaw St. D1
Shaw's Alley B4
Sir Thomas St. B3
Skelhorne St. C3
Slater St. C4
Smithfield St. B2
Soho St. D2
South John St. B3
Sparling St. B4/B5
Springfield St. D2
Stafford St. D2

Stanley St. B3
Strand St. B3/B4
Suffolk St. C4
Tabley St. B4
Tarleton St. C3
Temple St. B3
Titchfield St. B1
Tithebarn St. B2
Upr Duke St. D4
Upr Frederick St. C4
Upr Hope Pl. D4
Vandries St. A1
Vauxhall Rd. B1/B2

Vernon St. B2
Victoria St. B3
Village St. D1
Vulcan St. A1
Wapping B4
Water St. A3/B3
Waterloo Rd. A1/A2
Whitechapel B3
William Brown St. C2
William Henry St. D1
Wood St. C3/C4
York St. C4

On the Motorway

● If you have vehicle problems, try to drive to the next emergency telephone. If you have to walk, directional arrows on marker posts point to the nearest telephone.

● Switch on your hazard warning lights, and keep your sidelights on if it is dark or visibility is poor.

● Walk on the inside of the hard shoulder, and when you reach the phone, stand behind it facing on-coming traffic.

● Return to your car and lock all the doors except the passenger door. Stay on the embankment unless you feel there is an obvious danger.

● If an unidentified vehicle draws up, get back in the car and lock the door.

● If anyone offers to help, ask them to contact the appropriate emergency service, rather than assist personally.

● If you see another driver in difficulty, drive on and report it by telephone as soon as possible.

● Never pick up hitch-hikers.

45

London *West*

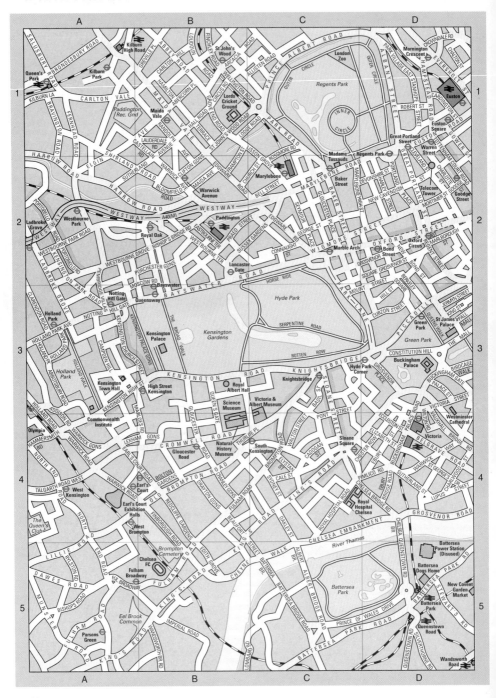

London *East*

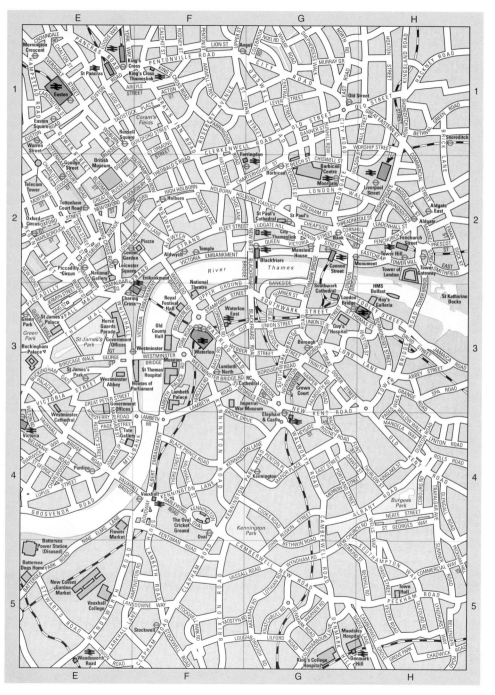

47

London *Index*

Abbey Rd. B1
Abbey St. H3
Abbotsbury Rd. A3
Abercorn Pl. B1
Arcacia Rd. B1
Acton St. F1
Addison Rd. A4
Akerman Rd. G5
Albany Rd. G4
Albany St. D1
Albert Bridge C5
Albert Bridge Rd. C5
Albert Embankment F4
Aldersgate G2
Aldwych F2
Allisten Rd. C1
Amwell St. F1
Argyle St. E1/F1
Baker St. C2
Balfour St. G4
Bankside G2
Banner St. G1
Basil St. C3
Battersea Bridge C5
Battersea Bridge Rd. C5
Battersea Park Rd. E5
Baylis Rd. F3
Bayswater Rd. B3/C2
Beaufort St. B4
Beech St. G2
Belgrave Rd. D4
Bell St. C2
Bellenden Rd. H5
Belvedere Rd. F3
Benhill Rd. H5
Berkeley Sq. D3
Bermondsey St. H3
Bethnal Gn. Rd. H1
Bethwin Rd. G5
Birdcage Walk E3
Bishop's Rd. A5
Bishop's Bridge Rd. B2
Bishopsgate H2
Black Prince Rd. F4
Blackfriars Bridge G2
Blackfriars Rd. G3
Bloomfield Rd. B2
Bloomsbury St. E2
Bloomsbury Way E2/F2
Bolton Gdns. B4
Bondway F4
Borough High St. G3
Borough Rd. G3
Bravington Rd. A1
Brick La. H1
Bridge Rd. H3
Brixton Rd. F5
Brompton Rd. C4
Brondesbury Rd. A1
Brook Dr. F4
Buckingham Gate E3
Buckingham Palace Rd. D4

Bunhill Row G1
Cadogan St. C4
Cale St. C4
Calshot St. F1
Camberwell Grove H5
Camberwell New Rd. G5
Camberwell Rd. G4/G5
Campden Hill A3
Cannon St. G2
Cardington St. D1
Carlton Hill B1
Carlton Vale A1
Castellain Rd., B1/B2
Central St. G1
Chadwick Rd. H5
Chalton St. E1
Chancery La. F2
Charing Cross Rd. E2
Charlotte St. E2
Charlwood St. E4
Charterhouse St. F2/G2
Cheapside G2
Chelsea Bridge D4
Chelsea Bridge Embankment C4
Chelsea Bridge Rd. C4/D4
Chester Row C4/D4
Cheyne Walk B5/C5
Chiswell St. G2
Church St. B2/C2
Circus Rd. B1
City Rd. G2
Clarendon Rd. A3
Clerkenwell Rd. F1/G1
Cleveland St. D2
Clifton Gdns. B2
Coburg Rd. H4
Coldharbour La. G5
Colebrook Rd. G1
Commercial St. H1/H2
Commercial Way H5
Connaught St. C2
Constitution Hill D3
Cooks Rd. G4
Cornhill G2
Cornwall Rd. F3
Cranley Gdns. B4
Cromwell Rd. B4
Crowndale Rd. E1
Curzon St. D3
Dawes Rd. A5
Dawes St. G4
Dean St. E2
Denmark Hill G5
Denmark Rd. G5
Devonshire St. D2
Dock St. H2
Drayton Gdns. B4
Druid St. H3
Drury La. F2
Dunton Rd. H4
Earl's Court Rd. A4/B4
East Rd. G1
East Smithfield H2
East St. G4

Eastbourne Ter. B2
Eastcheap H2
Ebury Bridge Rd. D4
Ebury St. D4
Eccleston St. D4
Edgware Rd. B2/C2
Edith Grove B5
Edmund St. G5
Elgin Ave. A2/B1
Elizabeth St. D4
Elystan St. C4
Embankment F2/F3
Euston Rd. D1/E1
Eversholt St. E1
Falmouth Rd. G3
Farringdon Rd. F1
Fenchurch St. H2
Fentiman Rd. F4/F5
Fernhead Rd. A1
Finborough Rd. B4
Finchley Rd. B1
Fleet St. F2
Flint St. G4
Frampton St. B2
Fulham Broadway A5
Fulham Rd. A5/B5/B4
George St. C2
Glengall Rd. H4
Gloucester Pl. C2
Gloucester Rd. B4
Goodge St. E2
Goods Way E1
Goswell Rd. G1
Gower St. E1/E2
Grange Rd. H3
Gray's Inn Rd. F1
Great Ormond St. F1
Gresham St. G2
Greville Pl. B1
Grosvenor Pl. D3
Grosvenor Rd. D4
Grosvenor Sq. D2
Grosvenor St. D2
Grove End Rd. B1
Grove La. H5
Grove Park H5
Gt. Dover St. G3
Gt. Eastern St. H1
Gt. George St. E3
Gt. Peter St. E3
Gt. Portland St. D2
Gt. Russell St. E2
Gt. Suffolk St. G3
Guildford St. F1
Hackney Rd. H1
Hall Rd. B1
Hamilton Ter. B1
Hammersmith Rd. A4
Hampstead Rd. E1
Harley St. D2
Harleyford Rd. F4
Harper Rd. G3
Harrow Rd. A2/B2
Hartington Rd. F5
Hatton Gdn. F2
Havil St. H5

Haymarket E2
Hercules Rd. F3
Heygate St. G4
High Holborn E2/F2
Hill St. D3
Holborn F2
Holborn Viaduct G2
Holland Park A3
Holland Park Ave. A3
Holland Rd. A3/A4
Holland Walk A3
Horseferry Rd. E4
Houndsditch H2
Hoxton St. H1
Imperial Rd. B5
Jamaica Rd. H3
Jermyn St. D3
John Islip St. E4
John Ruskin St. G4/G5
Judd St. E1
Kennington La. F4/G4
Kennington Oval F4
Kennington Park Rd. F4/G4
Kennington Rd. F4
Kensington Church St. A3/B3
Kensington High St. A3/A4
Kensington Park Rd. A2/A3
Kensington Rd. B3/C3
Kilburn La. A1
King St. D3
King's Cross Rd. F1
King's Rd. A5/B5/C4
Kinglake St. H4
Kingsland Rd. H1
Kingsway F2
Knatchbull Rd. G5
Knightsbridge C3
Ladbroke Grove A2/A3
Lambeth Bridge F4
Lambeth Palace Rd. F3
Lambeth Rd. F3
Lansdowne Way E5/F5
Larkhall La. E5
Lauderdale Rd. B1
Leadenhall St. H2
Leman St. H2
Lever St. G1
Lexham Gdns. A4/B4
Lilford Rd. G5
Lillie Rd. A5
Lisson Grove B1/C2
Lodge Rd. B1/C1
Lombard Rd. B5
London Bridge G2
London Rd. G3
London Wall G2/H2
Long Acre E2/F2
Lothian Rd. G5
Loudon Rd. B1
Loughborough Rd. F5/G5

Ludgate Hill G2
Lupus St. E4
Lyndhurst Way H5
Lynton Rd. H4
Maida Ave. B2
Maida Vale B1
Mandela Way H4
Manor Place G4
Mansell St. H2
Marlborough St. D2
Marloes Rd. A3/B4
Marsham St. E4
Marylebone High St. C2/D2
Marylebone Rd. C2
Merrow St. G4
Middlesex St. H2
Millbank E4
Moorgate G2
Mortimer St. E2
Moscow Rd. A2/B2
Mostyn Rd. F5
Mount St. C3/D3
Munster Rd. A5
Murray Grove G1
Neate St. H4
New Bond St. D2
New Bridge St. G2
New Cavendish St. D2
New Church Rd. G4/H4
New Kent Rd. G3
New Oxford St. E2
Newington Causeway G3
Nine Elms La. E4
Noel Rd. G1
North End Rd. A4
North Rd. G1
Notting Hill Gate A3
Oakley St. C4
Old Brompton Rd. B4
Old Kent Rd. H4
Old St. G1/H1
Oxford St. D2
Page St. E4
Pages Walk H3
Palace St. E3
Pall Mall E3
Pancras Rd. E1
Park La. C3/D3
Park Rd. C1
Park Village East D1
Paul St. H1
Peckham Hill St. H5
Peckham Rd. H5
Pembridge Villas A2/A3
Penton Pl. G4
Penton St. F1
Pentonville Rd. F1
Piccadilly Circus D3
Piccadilly D3
Pimlico Rd. D4
Pont St. C3/C4
Porchester Gdns. B2
Portland Pl. D2

Portland St. G4
Portobello Rd. A2
Praed St. B2/C2
Prescott St. H2
Prince Albert Rd. C1
Prince of Wales Dr. C5/D5
Queen Victoria St. G2
Queen's Gate B3/B4
Queen's Walk D3
Queenstown Rd. D5
Randolph Ave. B1/B2
Redcliffe Gdns. B4
Regency St. E4
Regent St. D2
Robert St. D1
Rodney Rd. G4
Rodney St. F1
Rolls Rd. H4
Roseberry Ave. F1
Rossmore Rd. C1/C2
Rotten Row C3
Royal Hospital Rd. C4
Russell Sq. E1
Rylston Rd. A5
Salusbury Rd. A1
Serpentine Rd. D3
Seymour Pl. C2
Shaftesbury Ave. E2
Shepherdess Walk G1
Shirland Rd. A2/B2
Shoe La. F2
Shoreditch High St. H1
Silverthorne Rd. D5
Sloane St. C3/C4
South Lambeth Rd. F4/F5
Southampton Row F2
Southampton Way H5
Southwark Bridge G2/G3
Southwark Bridge Rd. G3
Southwark St. CE
Spa Rd. H3
St. George's Rd. E3/G3
St. George's Way H4
St. George's Dr. D4
St. John's St. F1/G1
St. John's Wood Rd. B1
St. Thomas St. G3/H3
Stamford St. F3
Stanhope St. D1
Stewart's Rd. E5
Stockwell Park Rd. F5
Stockwell Rd. F5
Strand F2
Sumner Pl. H5
Sumner St. G3
Sussex Gdns. B2/C2
Sutherland Ave. A2/B1
Sutherland St. D4
Sydney St. C4
Talfourd Rd. H5
Talgarth Rd. West A4

Tavistock Pl. E1/F1
The Broad Walk B3
The Cut F3
The Mall E3
Theobald's Rd. F2
Threadneedle St. G2/H2
Thurloe Pl. B4/C4
Thurlow St. H4
Tooley St. H3
Tottenham Ct. Rd. E1/E2
Tower Bridge H2
Tower Bridge Rd. H3
Tower Hill H2
Trafalgar Avenue H4
Trafalgar Sq. E2/E3
Trinity St. G3
Tyers St. F4
Union Rd. E5
Union St. G3
Upper Ground F3
Upper St. F1
Vassal Rd. F5/G5
Vauxhall Bridge Rd. E4
Vauxhall St. F4
Victoria St. E3
Walton St. C4
Walworth Rd. G4
Wandsworth Bridge Rd. B5
Wandsworth Rd. E5
Wardour St. E2
Warner Rd. G5
Warwick Ave. B2
Warwick Gdns. A4
Warwick Rd. A4
Warwick Way D4
Waterloo Bridge F2/F3
Waterloo Rd. F3
Webber St. F3/G3
Wellington Rd. B1/C1
Wells Way H4
Westbourne Grove A2/B2
Westbourne Park Rd. A2
Westbourne Ter. B2
Westminster Bridge F3
Westminster Bridge Rd. F3
Weston St. H3
Westway A2/B2
Wharf Rd. G1
White Lion St. F1
Whitehall E3
Wigmore St. C2/D2
Willow Walk H3/H4
Wilson St. G2
Wilton Rd. D4
Woburn Pl. E1
Worship St. H1
Wyndham Rd. G5
York Rd. F3
York Way E1

What to carry in your car
Don't be at a loss if you break down or are involved in an accident.
The following items can be easily stored in your vehicle and will prove useful - torch, hazard
warning triangle, jump leads, tow rope, first aid kit, and blanket. In winter, always carry warm
clothing and a pair of wellington boots.

London *M25*

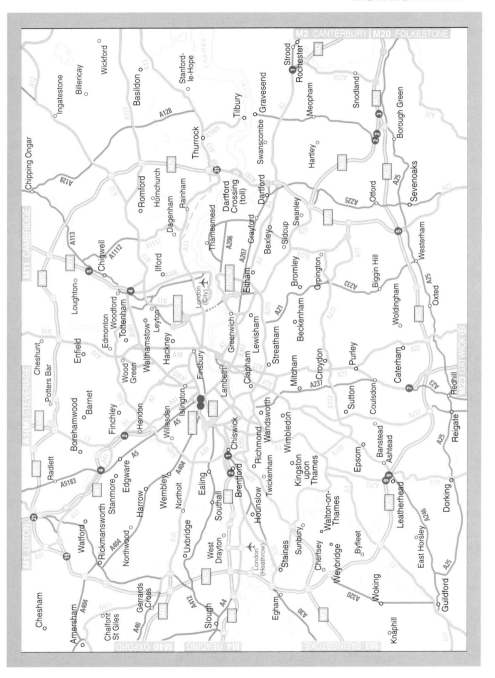

49

Manchester

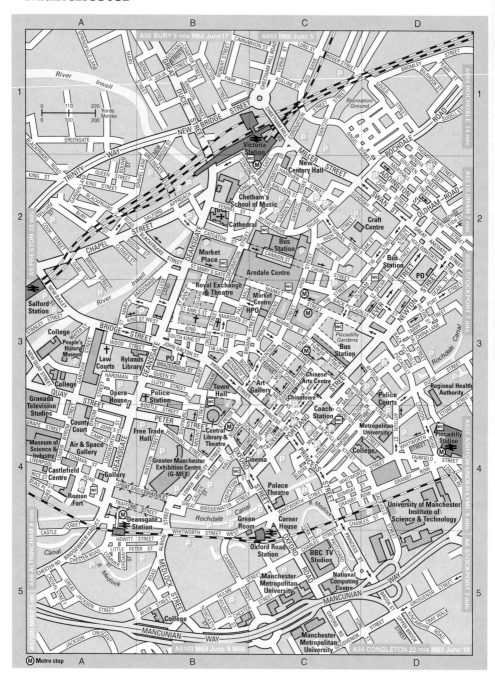

50

Manchester *Index*

Addington St. D2
Adeline St. C1
Albert Square B3
Albion St. B4/B5
Angel St. C1
Aytoun St. D3/D4
Back Piccadilly C3/D3
Balloon St. C2
Bendix St. D2
Berkeley St. B1
Bilbrook St. D1
Blackfriars Rd. A1/A2
Blackfriars St. B2
Bloom St. C4
Bombay St. C4
Booth St. A2
Booth St. B3/C3
Bootle St. C4
Bound St. A2
Bradshaw St. C2
Brazennose St. B3
Briddon St. D1
Bridge St. A3
Bridgewater V'duct A5
Bromley St. D1
Brook St. D5
Brown St. B3
Brown St. A2

Bury St. A2
Byrom St. A3/A4
Cable St. D2
Calder St. B4
Cambridge St. B5
Camp St. A4
Cannon St. C2
Carnarvon St. B1/C1
Castle St. A5
Cateaton St. B2
Chapel St. A2/B2
Charles St. C5/D4
Charlotte St. C3
Charter St. B1
Cheetham Hill Rd. C1
Chepstow St. B4
Chester Rd. A5
Chester St. B5/C5
China La. D3
Chorlton St. C4/D4
Church St. C2
City Rd. B5
Clowes St. A2
College Land B3
Commercial St. A5
Cook St. A2
Corporation St. B2/C1
Cray Walk D5
Cross St. B3

Crown St. A5
Dale St. D3
Dantzic St. C1/C2
Dean St. D3
Deansgate A3/B2
Dickinson St. B4/C4
Ducie St. D3
Duke Pl. A4
Duke St. A4
Dutton St. B1
East St. B4
Fairfield St. D4
Faulkner St. C4
Fennel St. B2
Fernie St. C1
Fountain St. C3
Garden La. A2
Garden St. C2
Gartside St. A3
George Leigh St. D2
George St. B3/B4
Goadsby St. C2/D2
Gould St. D1
Goulden St. D2
Granby Row D4
Grape St. A4
Gravel La. B2
Gt. Ancoats St. D2
Gt. Bridgewater St. A4/B4

Great Ducie St. B1
Great Jackson St. A5
Greengate B2
Grosvenor St. C5/D5
Hall St. B4
Hanover St. C2
Hardman St. A3
Henry St. D2
Hewitt St. A5/B5
High St. C3/C2
Hilton St. D2/D3
Houldsworth St. D2
Hulme St. B5
Jackson Cres. A5
John Dalton St. B3
Jordan St. A5
Julia St. B1
Kennedy St. B3
Kincardine Rd. D5
King St. A2
King St. B3
King St. West A3/B3
Lever St. D2/D3
Little Peter St. A5/B5
Liverpool Rd. A4
Lloyd St. B3
London Rd. D4
Long Millgate B2/C2
Longworth St. A4

Lord St. C1
Lower Byrom St. A4
Lower Mosley St. B4
Major St. C3/C4
Mancunian Way A5/D5
Marble St. C3
Market St. C3
Marsden St. B3
Marshall St. D2
Mary St. A1/B1
Medlock St. B5
Miller St. C2
Minshull St. C3/D4
Mosley St. C3
Mount St. B4
New Bailey St. A3
New Bridge St. B1
New Quay St. A3
Newcastle St. B5
Newton St. D3
Nicholas St. C4
Oak St. D2
Oldham Rd. D2/C4
Oldham St. C3/D4
Oxford Rd. C4/C5
Oxford St. B4/C4
Pall Mall B3
Park St. B1
Parker St. C3

Peary St. D1
Piccadilly D3
Port St. D3
Portland St. C3/C4
Princess St. B3/C5
Pritchard St. C5
Quay St. A2/A3
Queen St. A2
Queen St. B3
Red Bank C1
Rice St. A4
Richmond St. C4
River St. B5
Robert St. B1
Rochdale Rd. D1
Roger St. C1
St. Ann's Sq. B3
St. Ann's St. B3
St. James St. C4
St. John's St. A4
St. Mary's Gate B2
St. Mary's
St. Peter's Sq. B4
Sackville St. C4/D4
Salford Approach B2
Shudehill C2
South King St. B3
Southall St. B1

Southmill St. B4
Spear St. D2/D3
Spring Gardens C3
Springfield La. A1
Stanley St. A3
Station Approach B2
Store St. D3/D4
Sudell St. D1
Swan St. D2
Tariff St. D3
Thomas St. C2
Thompson St. D1/D2
Tib La. B3
Tib St. C2/D2
Tonman St. A4
Trafford St. A4/B4
Trinity Way A2
Turner St. C2
Upper Brook St. D5
Water St. A3
Watson St. B4
Whitworth St. C4/D4
Whitworth St. West B4
William St. A2
Windmill St. B4
Withy Grove C2
Wood St. A3
York St. C3
York St. C4/C5

Motoring and the Environment

Take a few simple measures to minimise the impact of your car on the environment and you'll also make significant savings in motoring costs.

- Choose your car with care, taking into account type of fuel, fuel consumption and engine size.
- Ensure your car is regularly serviced.
- Avoid heavy acceleration and braking.
- Keep within the speed limits.
- Select the right gear, getting into the highest gear as soon as possible.
- Don't carry unnecessary loads, and remove roof-racks when not in use.
- Avoid congestion wherever possible.
- Switch off the engine in severe traffic jams.
- Use public transport when possible.

51

Milton Keynes

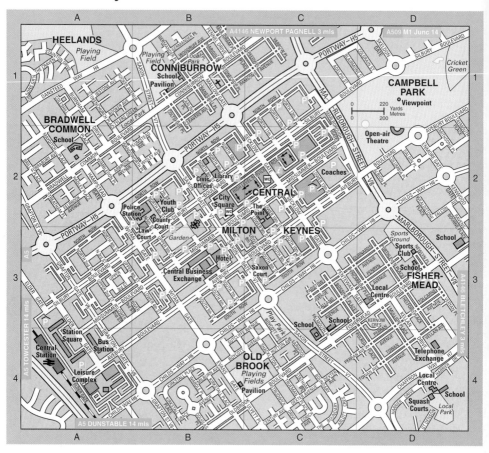

Adelphi St. C1
Albion Pl. D2
Arbrook Ave. A2
Arlott Cres. C4
Avebury Blvd. A4/D1
Blairmont St. C1
Booker Ave. A1
Bossiney Pl. C3
Boycott Ave. B4/C3
Bradwell Common Blvd. A2
Brill Pl. A2
Burnham Dr. A1
Carlina Pl. B1
Century Ave. C4
Chaffron Way (H7) D4
Childs Way (H6) A4/D2
Cleavers Ave. B1
Coleshill Pl. A1
Colgrain St. D1
Coltsfoot Pl. B1
Columbia Pl. D2

Conniburrow Blvd. B1
Cranesbill Pl. B1
Dalgin Pl. D2
Dansteed Way (H4) A1
Dexter Ave. C4
Douglas Pl. B4
Edrich Ave. C4
Eelbrook Ave. A2
Elder Gate A3/A4
Enmore Gate D2
Evans Gate B4
Falcon Ave. D2
Falmouth Pl. C4
Fennel Dr. B1
Fishermead Blvd. C3/D3
Forrabury Ave. A2
Germander Pl. B1
Gibsons Gn. A1
Grace Ave. B4
Grafton Gate (V6) A3/A4

Grafton Street (V6) A2
Grafton Street (V6) B4
Great Denson D4
Gurnards Ave. D3
Hadley Pl. A2
Hampstead Gate A2
Harrier Dr. D4
Helford Pl. D3
High Level Service Rd. B2/C2
Hutton Ave. C4
Ibstone Ave. A1
Kellan Dr. D3
Kenwood Gate D2
Kernow Cres. B3
Kirkstall Pl. B4
Larwood Pl. C4
Lower 2nd St. A3
Lower 3rd St. B3
Lower 4th St. B3

Lower 8th St. C3
Lower 9th St. C2
Lower 10th St. C2
Lower 12th St. C2
Mallow Gate B1
Marigold Pl. B1
Marjoram Pl. B1
Marlborough Gate C1
Marlborough Street (V8) C1/D3
Mayditch Pl. A2
Midsummer Blvd. A3/C2
Milburn Ave. B4
Mullion Pl. D3
Newlyn Pl. D3
North 2nd St. A3
North 3rd St. A3
North 4th St. A3
North 5th St. B2
North 6th St. B2
North 7th St. B2

North 8th St. B2
North 9th St. B2
North 10th St. B2
North 11th St. C1
North 12th St. C1
North 13th St. C1
North Row A3/C1
Oldbrook Blvd. B4
Padstow Ave. C3
Pencarrow Pl. C3
Penryn Ave. D3
Pentewan Gate C3
Perran Ave. C4/D4
Plumstead Ave. B2
Polruan Pl. D4
Porthleven Pl. D3
Portway (H5) A3/C1
Ramsons Ave. C1
Ravensbourne Pl. D2
Saxon Gate (V7) B2/C3
Saxon St. (V7) B1
Saxon St. (V7) C4

Secklow Gate C2/C3
Shackleton Pl. C4
Silbury Blvd. A3/D1
Skeldon Gate D1
Smithsons Pl. D2
South 5th St. B3
South 6th St. B3
South 7th St. B3
South 8th St. C3
South 9th St. C3
South 10th St. C3
South Row B3/C3
Speedwell Pl. C4
Stainton Dr. A1
Statham Pl. C4
Stokenchurch Pl. A1
Stonecrop Pl. B3
Streatham Pl. A2
Strudwick Dr. C4
Sutcliffe Ave. B4
Talland Ave. C3
Taymouth Pl. D1

The Boundary C4
The Craven A1
Tolcarne Ave. D3
Towan Ave. D4
Trueman Pl. C4
Tylers Gn. A1
Ulyett Pl. C4
Upper 2nd St. A3
Upper 3rd St. A3
Upper 4th St. A3
Upper 5th St. B3
Vellan Ave. D4
Veryan Pl. D3
Wandsworth Pl. A2
Wardle Pl. B4
Wealdstone Pl. D2
Wimbledon Pl. A2
Wisley Ave. B2
Witan Gate A3/B3
Woodruff Ave. B1
Yarrow Pl. C1

Newcastle upon Tyne

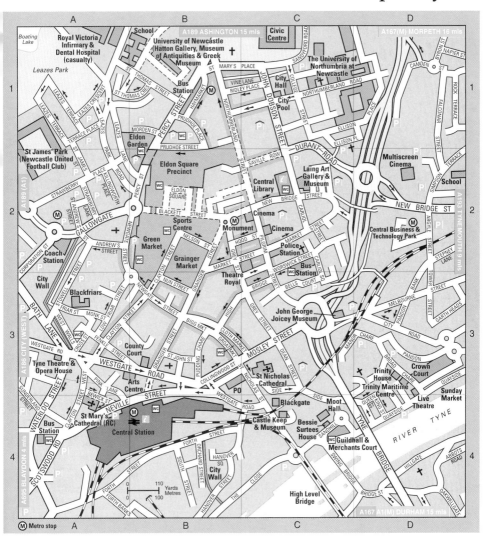

Abbot's Rd. D4	Cloth Market B3	Grainger St. B3	Leazes Ter. A1	Nun St. B3	St. Andrew's St. A2	Strawberry La. A2
Argyle St. D2	College St. C1	Grey St. B2/C3	Low Friar St. A3	Oakwellgate D4	St. James St. A2	Strawberry Pl. A2
Bath La. A3	Collingwood St. B3	Groat Market B3	Manor Chare C3	Orchard St. B4	St. John's St. B3	Sunderland St. A3/A4
Bells Court C3	Corporation St. A2	Hanover Sq. B4	Market St. B2/C2	Pandon D3	St. Mary's Pl. B1/C1	Swing Bridge C4
Bewick St. A3/A4	Cross St. A3	Hanover St. B4	Melbourne St. D3	Pandon Bank D3	St. Nicholas St. C3/C4	Terrace Pl. A1
Bigg Market B3	Durant Rd. C1/C2	Haymarket B1	Monk St. A3	Percy St. B1/B2	St. Thomas Cres. A1/B1	The Close B4/C4
Blackett St. B2	Eldon Sq. B2	High Bridge B3/C3	Morden St. A1/B1	Pilgrim St. C2/C3	St. Thomas St. A1/B1	Tower St. D3
Bridge St. D4	Ellison Pl. C1/D1	Hillgate D4	Mosley St. C3	Pink La. A3	Sandhill C4	Tyne Bridge C3/D4
Broad Chare D3	Falconar St. D1	Hood St. B2/C2	Napier St. D1	Prudhoe Pl. B1	Saville Row C2	Vine La. B1/C1
Byron St. D1	Fenkle St. A3	John Dobson St. C1	Nelson St. B2	Prudhoe St. B1	Scotswood Rd. A4	Waterloo St. A3/A4
Camden St. D1	Forth Banks A4	Killingworth Pl. A2	Neville St. A4/B3	Pudding Chare B3	Side C3	West Walls A3
Carliol Sq. C2	Forth St. A4/B4	King St. D4	New Bridge St. C2/D2	Quayside D3/D4	Simpson Ter. D2	Westgate Rd. A3/B3
City Rd. D3	Friars St. A3	Leazes Cres. A1	Newgate St. A2	Queen St. D4	South St. B4	Worswick St. C2
Clayton St. A3/B3	Gallowgate A2	Leazes La. A1/A2	Northumberland Rd. C1	Ridley Pl. B1/C1	Stepney La. D2	
Clayton St. West A3/A4	Garth Heads D3	Leazes Park Rd. A1/A2	Northumberland St. B1/C2	Rock Ter. D1	Stowell St. A2/A3	

Northampton

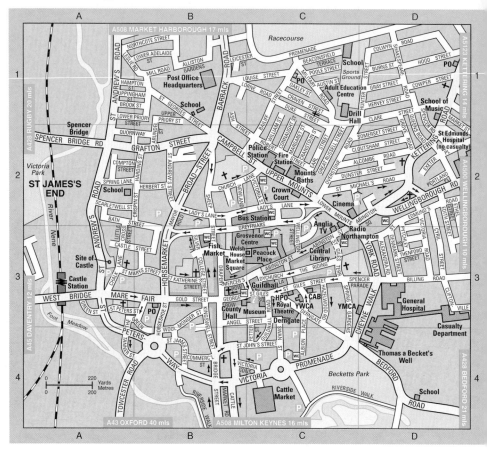

Abington Sq. D2	Cattle Market Rd. B4	Dunster St. C2	Horsemarket B3	Newland B2	Spring Gdns. C3	Upper Mounts.C2
Abington St. C3	Chalk La. A3	Dychurch La. C3	Horseshoe St. B3	Northcote St. B1	Spring La. A2	Upper Priory St. B1
Albion Pl. C4	Charles St. C1	Earl St. C2	Hunter St. D1	Oakley St. C1	St Andrew's Rd. A1/A3	Uppingham St. A1
Alcombe St. D2	Cheyne Walk.D3	Edith St. D2	Kettering Rd. D2	Overstone St. C2	St Andrew's St. B2	Victoria Gdns. B4
Alexandra Rd. D3	Church La. B2	Ethel St. D2	Kingswell St. B3	Peacock Pl. B3	St Edmund's Rd. D2	Victoria Promenade C4
Alliston Gdns. B1	Clare St. D1	Exeter Pl. D2	Lady's La. B2/C2	Peters Way B4	St Georges St. B1	Victoria Rd. D3
Angel St. B3	Cliftonville D3	Fetter St. C4	Leicester St. B1	Poole St. C1	St Giles Sq. C3	Victoria St. C2
Arundel St. B2	Cloutsham St. D2	George Row B3	Leslie Rd. A1	Portland Pl. D2	St Giles St. C3	Wellingborough Rd.
Ash St. B1	College St. B3	Gold St. B3	Little Cross St. A3	Promenade C1	St Giles Ter. C3	D2
Austin St. C1	Colwyn Rd. D1	Grafton St. B2	Lorne Rd. C1	Pytchley St. D3	St James St. B4	Wellington St. C3
Bailiff St. C1	Commercial St. B4	Gray St. D1	Louise St. C1	Queens Rd. D1	St John's St. C4	William St. C2
Barrack Rd. B1	Compton St. A2	Great Russell St. C2	Lower Adelaide St. B1	Quornway A2	St Katherine's St. B3	William St. C2
Bath St. A2	Connaught St. C2	Green St. A3	Lower Mounts C2	Riverside Walk B4/C4	St Marys St. A3	Woodford St. D3
Beaconsfield Ter. C1	Cowper St. D1	Greyfriars B3	Lower Priory St. A1	Robert St. C2	St Michael's Rd. C2	Wool Monger St. B4
Bedford Rd. D4	Cranstoun St. C2	Grove Rd. D2	Mare Fair A3	Scarletwell St. A2	St Peters St. A3	York Rd. D3
Billing Rd. D3	Craven St. C1	Guildhall Rd. C4	Margaret St. C2	Shakespeare Rd. D1	Swan St. C4	
Bridge St. B4	Crispin St. B2	Hampton St. A1	Market Sq. B3	Sheep St. B2	Tanner St. A4	
Broad St. B2	Cyril St. D3	Harding St. B2	Market St. D1	Silver St. B3	The Green A3/B3	
Brook St. A1	Denmark St. D3	Hazelwood Rd. C3	Mayor Hold B2	Somerset St. D2	The Riding C3	
Burns St. D1	Derngate C3	Herbert St. B2	Mercer's Row B3	Spencer Bridge Rd. A2	Thenford St. D3	
Campbell St. B2	Drapery B3	Hervey St. D1	Military Rd. C1	Spencer Pde. C3	Thomas St. C2	
Castle St. A3	Duke St. C1	Hood St. D1	Mill Rd. B1	Spencer Rd. D1	Towcester Rd. A4	

Norwich

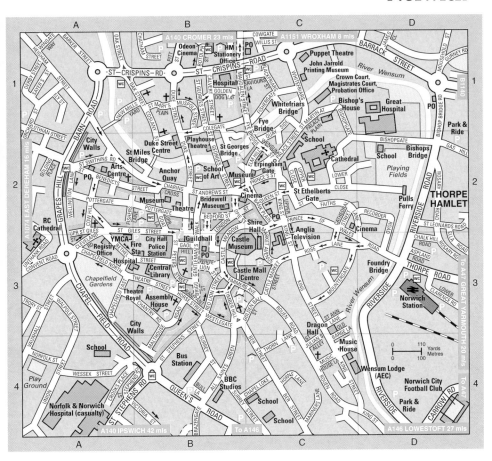

All Saints Gn. B4	Cattle Market St. C3	Ely St. A1	Lower Close C2	Prince's St. C2	St. Giles St. B2	Upper Cl. C2
Aspland Rd. D3	Chalk Hill Rd. D3	Farmers Ave. B3	Magdalen St. B1	Quay Side C1/C2	St. Julian's Alley C4	Upper Goat La. B2
Bank Plain C2	Chantry Rd. B3	Fishergate C1	Malthouse Rd. B3/B4	Queen St. C2	St. Leonards Rd. D2	Upper King St. C2
Barker St. A1	Chapel Field Rd. A3	Fishers La. A2	Mariners La. C4	Queen's Rd. B4	St. Martin at	Upper St. Giles St. A2
Barn Rd. A1	Chapel Loke C4	Fye Bridge C1/C2	Market Ave. C3	Rampant Horse St. B3	Palace Plain C1	Vauxhall St. A3/A4
Barrack St. D1	Chapelfield East A3	Gaol Hill B3	Mountergate C3	Recorder Rd. D2/D3	St. Mary's Plain B1	Victoria St. B4
Bedford St. B2	Chapelfield North A3	Gas Hill D2	Mousehold St. D1	Red Lion St. B3	St. Peters St. B3	Walpole St. A3
Ber St. C4	Charing Cross B2	Gentleman's Walk B3	Music House La. C4	Riverside Rd. D2	St. Saviours La. C1	Wellington La. A2
Bethel St. A3	Chatham St. B1	Golden Ball St. C3	Muspole St. B1	Riverside D3/D4	St. Stephens Rd. A4	Wensum St. C2
Bishop Bridge Rd. D1	Cleveland Rd. A3	Golden Dog La. B1	New Mills Yard A1	Rosary Rd. D2/D3	St. Stephens Sq. A4	Wessex St. A4
Bishopgate C1/D2	Colegate B1	Golding Pl. A2	Norfolk St. A4	Rose La. C3	St. Stephens St. B3/B4	Westlegate B3
Blackfriars St. C1	Convent Rd. A3	Grapes Hill A2	Oak St. A1/B1	Rouen La. C3/C4	St. Swithins Rd. A2	White Lion St. B3
Botolph St. B1	Coslany St. B1/2	Gurney Rd. D1	Old Barge La. C3/C4	Sayer's St. A1	Surrey St. B4/C4	Whitefriars C1
Brazengate B4	Cow Hill A2	Heigham St. A1	Opie St. B2	St. Andrews St. B2	Theatre St. B3	Willis St. C1
Brigg St. B3	Cowgate C1	Horns La. C4	Orchard St. A1	St. Ann La. C3	Thorn La. C4	Wingate Way A1
Bull La. B4	Crooks Pl. A4	James Cl. D1	Palace St. C2	St. Benedicts St. A2	Thorpe Rd. D3	
Calvert St. B1	Derby St. A1	King St. C2/D4	Pitt St. B1	St. Crispins Rd. A1/B1	Timber Hill B3	
Carrow Rd. D4	Duke St. B1/B2	London St. B2	Pottergate A2/B2	St. Faiths La. C2	Trory St. B3	
Castle Meadow B3	Ella Rd. D3	Lothian St. A1/A2	Prince of Wales Rd.	St. Georges St. B1/B2	Union St. A4	
Cathedral St. C2	Elm Hill C2	Lwr Clarence Rd. D3	C2/D3	St. Giles St. A2/B2	Unthank Rd. A3	

Nottingham

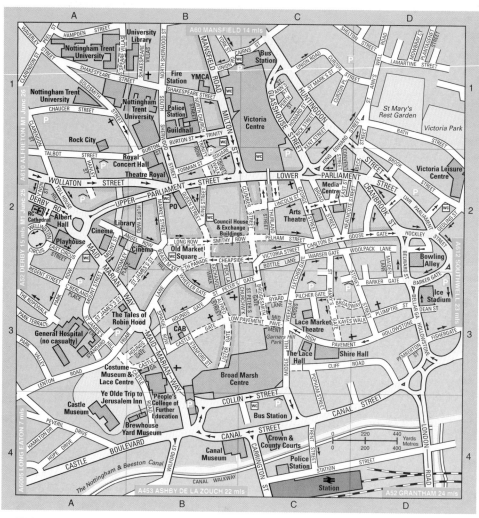

Alfred St. B3
Angel Row A2/B2
Barker Gate D3
Bath St. D1
Beast Market Hill B2
Beck St. D1/D2
Bellar Gate D3
Belward St. D2
Bottle La. C2
Bridgesmith Gate C3
Broad St. C2
Broadway C3
Bromley Pl. A2/A3
Brook St. B2
Burton St. B2/B1
Byard La. C3
Cairns St. C1
Canal St. B4/C4
Carlton St. C2
Carrington St. C4

Castle Blvd. A4/B4
Castle Gate B3
Castle Rd. D3
Castle Rd. B3/B4
Chaucer St. A1
Cheapside B2
Clarendon St. A1
Cliff Rd. C3/D3
Clumber St. C2
Collin St. B4/C4
Convent St. C2
Cranbrook St. D2
Cumberland Pl. A3
Curzon Pl. C1
Curzon St. C1
Dean St. D3
Derby Rd. A2
East Circus St. A2
East St. C2
Exchange Walk B3
Fishergate D3

Fletcher Gate C2/C3
Forman St. B2
Friar La. A3/B3
Gedling St. D2
George St. C2
Glasshouse St. C1
Goldsmith St. A1
Goose Gate D2
Hamilton Dr. A4
Hampden St. A1
Heathcote St. C2
High Pavement C3
Hockley St. D2
Hollowstone D3
Hope Dr. A4
Hounds Gate B3
Howard St. C1
Huntingdon St. C1/D2
Hurts Yard B2
Kayes Walk C3/D3

Kent St. C1
King Edward St. C1/C2
King St. B2
Lamartine St. D1
Lenton Rd. A3
Lincoln St. C2
Lister Gate B3
London Rd. D4
Long Row B2
Low Pavement B3/C3
Lwr Parliament St. C2/D2
Maid Marian Way A2/B3
Maiden La. D2
Mansfield Rd. B1
Market St. B2
Mid Pavement C3
Milton St. B1
Mount St. A3
Mowbray Court D1

Nth Church St. B1
Nth Sherwood St. B1
Park Row A3
Park Ter. A3
Park Valley A3
Peck La. B2/B3
Peel St. A1
Pelham St. C2
Pemberton St. D3
Perth St. C1
Peveril Dr. A4
Pilcher Gate C3
Plantagenet St. D1
Plumptre St. D3
Popham St. C3/C4
Queen St. B2
Regent St. A3
Rick St. C1
St. Ann's St. C1
St. Ann's Well Rd. D1

St. James's St. A3/B3
St. James's Ter. A3
St. Mark's St. C1
St. Mary's Gate C3
St. Peter's Gate B3/C3
St. Peter's Ch. Wlk C3
Shakespeare St. A1/B1
Shakespeare Villas A1/B1
Shelton St. C1/D1
Smithy Row B2
South Pde. B2
Sth Sherwood St. B1
Spaniel Row B3
Standard Hill A3
Stanford St. B3
Station St. C4/D4
Stoney St. D3
Talbot St. A2
The Ropewalk A3
Thurland St. C2

Toll House Hill A2
Trent St. C4
Trinity Row B1/B2
Trinity Walk B2
Trinity Sq. B1/B2
Union Rd. B1
Union Rd. C1
Upr Parliament St. A2/B2
Vernon St. A2
Victoria St. C2
Warser Gate C2
Waverley St. A1
Weekday Cross C3
Wellington Circus A2
Wheeler Gate B3
Wilford Rd. B4
Wilford St. B4
Wollaton St. A2
Woolpack La. D2
York St. B1

Oxford

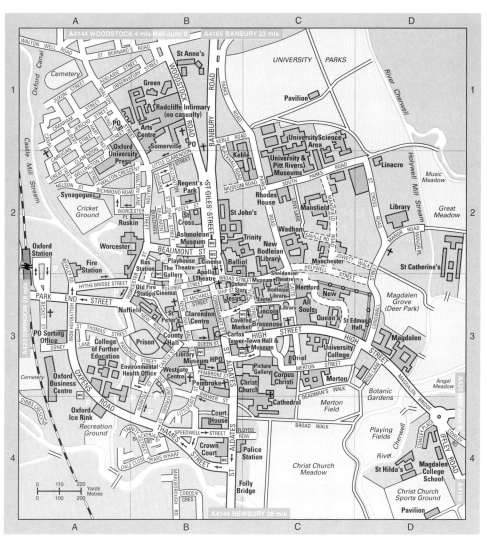

Adelaide St. A1
Albert St. A1/A2
Banbury Rd. B1
Beaumont Build'gs B2
Beaumont St. B2
Beckett St. A3
Black Rd. B4
Blackhall Rd. B1/B2
Broad St. B3/C3
Broad Walk C4
Canal St. A1/A2
Cardigan St. A1/A2
Castle St. B3

Catte St. C3
Cobden Cres. B4
Cornmarket St. B3
Cowley Pl. D4
Cowley Rd. D4
Cranham St. A1
Dale Cl. A4
Deadman's Walk C3
Floyds Row B4
Friars Wharf B4
George St. B3
Gibbs Cres. A4
Gt. Clarendon St. A1/A2

Hart St. A1
High St. C3
Hollybush Row A3
Holywell St. C2
Hythe Bridge St. A3
Iffley Rd. D4
Jericho St. A1
Jowett Walk C2/D2
Juxon St. A1
Keble Rd. B1
King St. A1
Kingston Rd. A1
Lit. Clarendon St. B2

Littlegate St. B4
Longwall St. D3
Love La. C2
Magdalen Bridge D3
Manor Pl. D2
Manor Rd. D2
Mansfield Rd. C2
Marlborough Rd. B4
Merton St. C3
Museum Rd. B2/C2
Nelson St. A2
New Inn Hall St. B3
New Rd. B3

Norfolk St. B3/B4
Observatory St. A1/B1
Old Greyfriars St. B4
Osney La. A3
Oxpens Rd. A3/A4
Paradise St. A3/B3
Park End St. A3
Parks Rd. B1/C2
Pembroke St. B3
Pusey St. B2
Queen St. B3
Rewley Rd. A2/A3
Richmond Rd. A2

Rose La. D3
St. Aldates B3/B4
St. Bernard's Rd. A1
St. Cross Rd. D2
St. Giles B2
St. John St. B2
St. Michael's St. B3
St. Thomas' St. A3
Saville Rd. C2
Ship St. B3
South Parks Rd. C2
Speedwell St. B4
Thames St. B4

Trinity St. B4
Turl St. C3
Walton Cres. A2
Walton La. B2
Walton St. A1/B2
Walton Well Rd. A1
Well Sq. B2
Wellington St. B2
Woodstock Rd. B1
Worcester Pl. A2
Worcester St. A3/B2

Peterborough

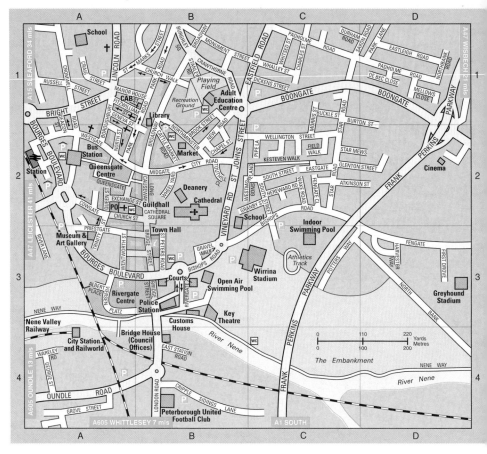

Albert Pl. A3	Cattle Market Rd. B2	East Station Rd. B4	Granby St. C2	New Rd. B2	Rivergate. B3	Wareley Rd. A4
Atkinson St. C2	Chapel St. B2	Eastfield Rd. C1	Gravel Walk B3	North Bank D3	Russell St. A1	Wellington St. C2
Bishops Rd. B3/C2	Charles St. C1	Eastgate C2	Grove St. A4	North St. A2	Saxon Rd. D1	Wentworth St. A3
Boongate C1/D1	Church St. A2	Eastleigh Rd. D1	Harvester Way D3	Northbank Rd. D1	South St. C2	Westgate. A2
Boroughbury A1/A2	Church Walk B1	Exchange St. A2	Hereward Rd. C2	Northminster B2	St Johns St. B2	Westmoreland Gdns.
Bourges Blvd. A2/A3	City Rd. B2	Fengate. D3	Kesteven Walk C2	Oundle Rd. A4	St Marks St. B1	B2
Bread St. A4	Cowgate A2	Fengate Cl. C2	Lincoln Rd. A1	Padholme Rd. C1/D1	St Peters Rd. B3	Whalley St. C1
Bridge St. B3	Craig St. A1	Field Walk C2	London Rd. B4	Park La. D1	Stanley Rd. B1	Wheel Yard B2
Bright St. A1	Crawthorne Rd. B1	First Drove D3	Long Causeway B2	Park Rd. A2/B1	Star Mews C2	Whitsed St. C1
Broadway B1/B2	Cripple Sidings La. B4	Fitzwilliam St. A1	Manor House St. A1	Pipe La. C2	Star Rd. C1/C2	
Brook St. B2	Cromwell Rd. A1	Frank Perkins	Mellows Cl. D1	Potters Way C3	Touthill Cl. B2	
Buckle St. C1	De Bec St. D1	Parkway C4/D2	Midgate B2	Priestgate A3	Trinity St. A3	
Burghley Sq. B1	Deacon St. A1	Geneva St. A1	Monument St. B1	Queen St. A2	Viersen Platz A3	
Burton St. C1/D1	Dickens St. C1	George St. A4	Morris St. C1	Queensgate A2	Vineyard Rd. B2	
Cathedral Sq. B2	Durham Rd. C1	Glenton St. C2	Nene Way A3-D4	River La. A3	Wake Rd. C2	

Plymouth

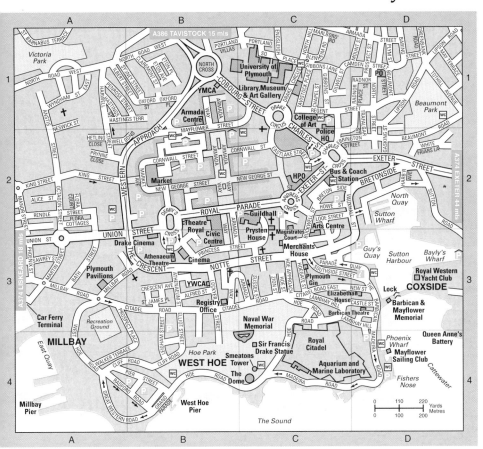

Alfred St. B3
Alice St. A2
Anstis St. A1/A2
Athenaeum St. B3
Armada St. D1
Armada Way B1/B2
Armada Way C3
Baring St. D1
Bath St. A3
Beaumont Rd. D2
Beaumont St. D1
Blenheim Rd. C1
Bretonside C2/D2
Buckwell St. C2
Camden St. D1
Chapel St. C1

Charles Cross C2
Charles St. C2
Citadel Rd. B3/C3
Citadel Rd. East C3
Claremont St. B1
Cliff Rd. A4/B4
Coburg St. B1
Cornwall St. B2/C2
Crescent Ave. B3
Derry's Cross B2
Drake Circus C1
Eastlake St. C2
Ebrington St. D1
Elliot St. B3
Endsleigh Pl. C1
Eton Ave. B1
Eton Pl. B1

Exeter St. C2/D2
Flora Cottages A2
Flora Court A2
Gasking St. D2
Gibbons La. C1
Gibbons St. C1
Gilwell St. C1
Grand Pde. B4
Gt. Western Rd. A4
Greenbank Rd. D1
Harbour Ave. D2
Harwell St. A1/A2
Hastings St. A1
Hastings Ter. A1
Hetling Cl. A2
Hoe Approach C3
Hoe Rd. B4/C3

Hoe St. C3
Hoegate St. C3
Howe St. C2
Ilbert St. A1
King St. A2
Lambhay Hill C3/D3
Leigham St. B4
Lipson Rd. D1
Lockyer St. B3
Looe St. C2
Madeira Rd. C4/D4
Manor St. A2
Market Ave. B2
Marlborough Rd. C1
Martin St. A3
May Ter. D1
Mayflower St. B1

Millbay Rd. A3
Mount St. D1
Neswick St. A1
New George St. B2/C2
New St. C3
North Cross B1
North Hill C1
North St. D1
North Rd. West A1/B1
Notte St. B3/C3
Octagon St. A2
Oxford Pl. B1
Oxford St. B1
Parade Quay C3
Penrose St. A3
Phoenix St. A3
Pier St. B4

Plym St. D1
Portland Sq. C1
Portland Villas B1
Princess St. B3
Prospect Pl. A3
Prospect St. D1
Prynne Cl. A2
Radford Rd. A4/B4
Radnor Pl. D1
Radnor St. D1
Regent St. C1
Rendle St. A2
Royal Pde. B2/C2
Sawrey St. A3
Southside St. C3
St. Andrews Cross C2
St. Barnabus Ter. A1

St. James Pl. B3
Sussex St. C3
Sutton Rd. D2
Sydney St. B1
Tavistock Pl. C1
The Barbican D3
The Crescent B3
Tothill Ave. D1
Trafalgar St. D1
Union St. A3/B3
Vauxhall St. C2
Walker Ter. A4
Well Gdns. A2
West Hoe Rd. A3/A4
Western App. A2/B1
Wyndham St East A1
Zion St. C3

Portsmouth

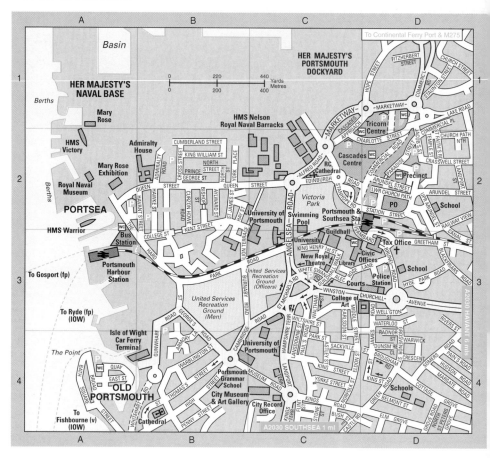

Admiralty Rd. B2
Alec Rose La. C3
Alfred Rd. C2
Angelsea Rd. C2/C3
Armory Ln. B3/B4
Arundel St. D2
Astley St. C4
Aylward St. B2
Bath Sq. A4
Belmont St. D4
Bishop St. B2
Broad St. A4
Brougham Rd. D4
Burnaby Rd. C3/B3
Bush St. East C4
Cambridge Rd. B4/C3
Castle Rd. C4
Charlotte St. D2

College St. B3
Commercial Rd. D1
Cottage Grove D4
Crasswell St. D2
Cross St. B2
Cumberland St. B1
Curzon Howe Rd. B2
Dunsmore Cl. D4
Earlsdon St. C3
East St. A4
Edinburgh Rd. C2
Elm Grove D4
Flint St. C4
Green Rd. D4
Grosvenor St. D3/D4
Guildhall Walk C3
Gunwharf Rd. B3/B4
Hampshire Ter. C3/C4

Havant St. B2
Hawke St. B2
Hay St. B2
High St. B4
Hyde Park Rd. D3
Isambard
Brunel Rd. C2/D3
Jacob's St. D1/D2
Kent St. B2
King Charles St. B4
King Henry 1st St. C3
King St. C4/D4
King William St. B2
King's Rd. C4
Kings Ter. C4
Landport Ter. C4
Lansdowne St. C3/C4
Lion Ter. B3

Lower Church Path D2
Marketway D1
Middle St. C3/C4
Museum Rd. C4
North St. B2
Paradise St. D2
Park Rd. B3/C3
Park St. C4
Penny St. B4
Prince George St. B2
Quay A4
Queen St. B2/C2
Radnor St. D3/D4
St. George's Rd. B3/B4
St. James Rd. D3/D4
St. James St. B2
St. Michael's Rd. C3
St. Paul's Rd. C3/C4

St. Thomas's St. B4
Sackville St. C4/D4
Somers Rd. D4
Stanhope Rd. C2
Station St. D2
Stone St. C4
Temple St. D2
The Hard A2/B3
Waltham St. C3
Warblington St. B4
Warwick Cres. D4
Waterloo St. D3
Wellington St. D3
White Swan Rd. C3
Whitehart Rd. A4/B4
Wiltshire St. C3
York Pl. B2
Yorke St. C4

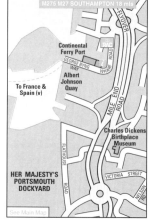

60

Ramsgate

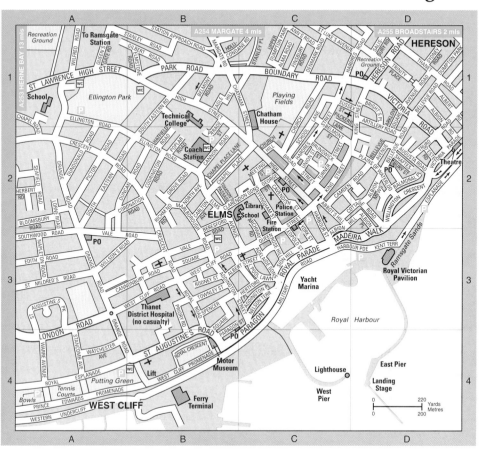

Abbot's Hill C2	Beresford Rd. B2	Denmark Rd. C1	Herbert Rd. A2	Paragon.C3	South Eastern Rd.	Turner St. C2
Addington Pl. C3	Bloomsbury Rd. A2	D'este Rd. D2	Hereson Rd. D1	Park Rd. B1	A2/B1	Union St. C2
Addington St. B3	Boundary Rd. C1	Dumpton Park D1	Hertford Pl. C3	Picton Rd. A2	Southwood Rd. A3	Upper Dumpton
Adelaide Gdns. C3	Bright's Pl. D1	Duncan Rd. A2/B2	High St. B1/C2	Plains of Waterloo.D2	Spencer Sq. B3	Park.C1
Albert Rd. D1	Broad St. C2	Dundonald Rd. A2	Hollicondane Rd. B1	Poplar Rd. B2	St Augustine's Rd. B4	Vale Rd. A3
Albert St. B3	Brunswick St. C2	Eagle HillB1	Kent Ter. D3	Prince Edwards	St Augustine's Park A3	Vale Sq. B3
Albion Mews D2	Camden Rd. C2	Edith Rd. A3	King St. C2/D2	Promenade A4	St Lawrence High St.	Victoria Pde. D2
Albion Pl. D2	Cannon Rd. B2	Effingham St. C2	Leopold St. C3	Priory Rd. B3	A1	Victoria Rd. D1
Albion Rd. D1	Cannonbury Rd. A3/B3	Ellington Rd. A1/B2	Liverpool Lawn C3	Queen St. C3	St Luke's Ave. C1	Warre Ave. A4
Alma Rd. C1	Carlton Ave. B2	Elms Ave. B2	London Rd. A4	Queen's Gate Rd. A1	St Mildred's Rd. A3	Watchester Ave. A4
Ann's Rd. C1	Cavendish St. C2	Elmstone Rd. B1	Lorne Rd. A2	Richmond Rd. B2	Stancomb Ave. A4	Wellington Cres. D2
Archway Rd. C2/3	Chapel Place La. B2	EsplanadeD2	Maderia Walk C3/D3	Rodney St. B3	Stanley Pl. C1	West Cliff Promenade
Arklow Sq. D1	Chapel Pl. B2	Finsbury Rd. C1	Margate Rd. B1	Rose Hill C3	Stanley Rd. B1	B4
Artillery Rd. D1	Chapel Rd. A1	George St. C2	Marlborough Rd. B2	Royal Cres. B4	Station Approach Rd.	West Cliff Rd. B3
Augusta Rd. D2	Chatham St. B1/C1	Gilbert Rd. B1	Meeting St. C2	Royal Esplanade A4	B1	Western Undercliff A4
Avenue Rd. D1	Church Hill C2	Grange Rd. A2/A4	Military Rd. C3	Royal Pde. C3	Sussex St. C1	Wilfred Rd. A1
Balmoral Rd. D2	Church Rd. C1	Grove Rd. B2	Napleton Rd. A3	Royal Rd. B3	Sydney Rd. D1	Willson's Rd. A3
Bellevue Ave. D2	Clarendon Gdns. B2/C2	Harbour Pde. C3/D3	Nelson Ter. C3	Salisbury Rd. D1	Thanet Rd. D1	York St. C3
Bellevue Rd. D1/D2	Codrington Rd. B2	Harbour St. C2	North Ave. B2	School La. C2	Tomson's Passage B2	
Belmont Rd. B1	Coronation Rd. B2	Hardres Rd. C1/D1	Packers La. C1	Seafield Rd. A2	Townley St. B3	
Belmont St. C2	Cottage Rd. D2	Hardres St. C2	Parade St. B2	Shaftesbury St. D2	Trinity Pl. D1	
	Crescent Rd. A2/B3	Hatfield Rd. B2	Paragon St. B4	Sion Hill C3	Truro Rd. D2	

Reading

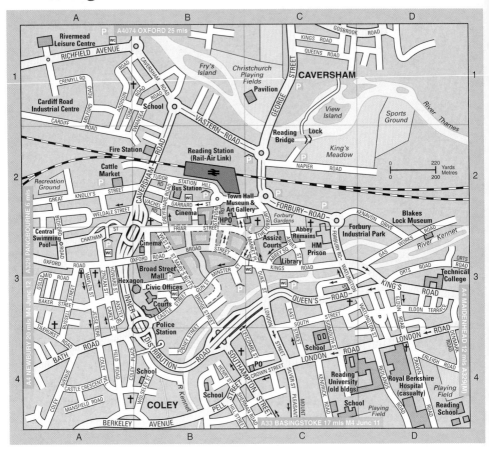

Abbey Sq. C3	Caversham Rd. B1/B2	Field Rd. A4	Howard St. A3	Market Pl. C3	Sherman Rd. B4/C4	Vastern Rd. B1/2
Abbey St. C3	Chatham St. A3	Fobney St. B4	Inner Distribution	Milford Rd. A1	Sidmouth St. C4	Watlington St. C3/D3
Addison Rd. A1	Coley Ave. A4	Forbury Rd. C2/C3	Rd. A3/B4	Minster St. B3	Silver St. C4	Waylen St. A3
Anstey Rd. A3	Coley Hill A4	Friar St. B3	Jesse Ter. A3	Mount Pleasant C4	South St. C3	Weldale St. A2
Baker St. A3	Coley Pl. A4	Garrard St. B2	Kenavon Dr. D2	Napier Rd. C2	Southampton St B4/C4	West St. B3
Bath Rd. A4	Craven Rd. C4	Gas Works Rd. D3	Kendrick Rd. C4	Orts Rd. D3	St. Mary's Butts B3	Wolseley St. B4
Bedford Rd. A2/A3	Cremyll Rd. A1	George St. C1	Kennet Side. D3	Oxford Rd. A3/B3	Station Hill B2	York Rd. A1/B1
Berkeley Ave. A4/B4	Crown St. C4	Goldsmid Rd. A3	King's Rd. C3/D3	Pell St. B4	Station Rd. B2	Zinzan St. A3
Bridge St. B3	Denmark Rd. D4	Gosbrook Rd. C1/D1	Kings Rd. (Caversham)	Queen's Rd. C3	Swansea Rd. B1	
Broad St. B3	Duke St. C3	Great Knolly's St. A2	C1	Queens Rd.	Thames Side B1	
Cardiff Rd. A1/A2	East St. C3/C4	Greyfriars Rd. B2	Letcombe St. C4	(Caversham) C1	The Forbury C2	
Carey St. A3	Eldon Rd. D3	Gun St. B3	London Rd. C4/D4	Redlands Rd. D4	Tilehurst Rd. A4	
Castle Cres. A4	Eldon Ter. D3	Henry St. B4	London St. C3/C4	Richfield Ave. A1	Tudor Rd. B2	
Castle St. B3	Erleigh Rd. D4	Hill St. B4	Mansfield Rd. A4	Russell St. A3	Vachel Rd. B2	

Slow down and save money

Keeping to the speed limits makes economic and environmental sense, and ensures you don't have a brush with the law. The most efficient, fuel-saving speed is between 50 and 60mph. At 70mph, your fuel costs and toxic emissions increase by at least 25%.

Salisbury

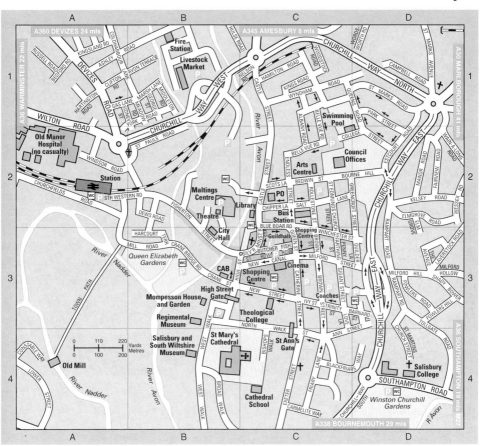

Albany Rd. C1	Carmelite Way C4	Crane St. B3	Gigant St. C3	Marsh La. B1	Rampart Rd. D2/D3	St Pauls Rd. B2
Ann St. C4	Castle St. C1/C2	Devizes Rd. A1	Greencroft St. C2	Meadow Rd. B1	Rollestone St. C2	The Avenue D3
Ashley Rd. A1	Catherine St. C3	Dews Rd. B2	Guilder La. D3	Middleton Rd. B1	Russell Rd. A1	Tollgate Rd. D3
Avon Ter. B1	Chipper La. C2	Elm Grove D2	Hamilton Rd. C1	Milford Hill D3	Salt La. C2	Town Path A3
Barnard St. D3	Churchfields Rd. A2	Elmgrove Rd. D2	Harcourt Ter. B3	Milford St. C3	Scots La. C2	Trinity St. C3
Bedford Rd. A1	Churchill Way East D2/D4	Endless St. C2	Hartington Rd. A1	Milford Hollow D3	Shady Bower D3	Wain-a-Long Rd. D2
Bedwin St. C2	Churchill Way North C1	Estcourt Rd. D2	High St. B3	Mill Rd. B3	Sidney St. A1	Wessex Rd. D2
Belle Vue Rd. C1/C2	Churchill Way South C4	Exeter St. C4	Hulse Rd. B1	Minster St. C3	Silver St. C3	West Walk B3/B4
Bishops Walk C4	Churchill Way West B1	Fairview Rd. D2	Ivy St. C3	Nelson Rd. C1	South Western Rd. A2	Wilton Rd. A1
Blackfriars Way C4	Clifton Rd. A1	Fish Row C3	Kelsey Rd. D2	New Canal C3	Southampton Rd. D4	Winchester St. C3
Blue Boar Rd. C2	Coldharbour La. A1	Fisherton St. B2	Kings Rd. C1	New St. C3	St Edmunds Church St. C2	Windsor Rd. A2
Bourne Hill C2	College St. C2	Fowlers Hill D3	Kingsland Rd. A1	North Walk St. C3	St Marks Avenue D1	Woodstock Rd. C1
Broad Walk B4	Constable Way A4	Fowlers Rd. D3	Laverstock Rd. D3	Park St. D1	St Marks Rd. D1	Wordsworth Rd. D1
Brown St. C3	Crane Bridge Rd. B3	Friary La. C4	Love La. C3	Penny Farthing St. C3	St Martins Church St. D4	Wyndham Rd. C1
Butcher Row C3		Gas La. A1	Lower St. A4	Queen St. C3		York Rd. B1
Campbell Rd. D1		George St. B1	Manor Rd. D2	Queens Rd. C1		

63

Scarborough

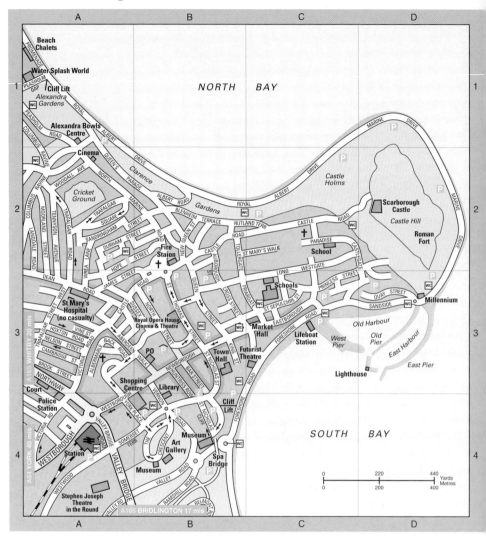

Aberdeen Walk A3/B3
Albermarle Back Rd. A3
Albert Rd. B2
Auborough St. B2
Bar St. B3
Belmont Rd. B4
Blenheim Ter. B2
Brook St. A3
Cambridge St. A3
Castle Rd. A3/D2

Castlegate C2/D2
Columbus Ave. A2
Columbus Ravine A1/A2
Cross St. B3
Dean Rd. A3
Durham St. A2/B2
Eastborough C3
Foreshore Rd. B4/C3
Friargate C3
Hope St. A2
Hoxton Rd. A3

Huntriss Row B3
James St. A3
King St. B3
Langdale Rd. A2
Long Westgate C2
Marine Dr. D1/D2
Moorland St. A2
Nelson St. A3
New Queen St. B2
Newborough B3
Nth Marine Rd. A2/B2

North St. B3
Northway A3
Paradise C2
Peasholm Gap A1
Peasholme Rd. A1
Princess St. C3
Promenade A1
Quay St. D3
Queen St. B3
Queen's Pde. A2
Ramshill Rd. B4

Royal Albert Dr. A1/C2
Rutland Ter. B2/C2
Sandringham St. A2
Sandside D3
Somerset Ter. A4
St. Mary's Walk C2
St. Nicholas Cliff B4
St. Nicholas St. B3
St. Sepulchre St. C3
St. Thomas St. B3
Sussex St. B3

Tennyson Ave. A2
The Crescent B4
Tollergate B2
Trafalgar Rd. A2
Trafalgar Sq. A2
Trafalgar St. West A3
Valley Bridge A4
Valley Bridge Rd. A4
Valley Rd. A4/B4
Vernon Rd. B4
Victoria Rd. A3/A4

Vine St. A3
Westborough A4
Westwood A4
Woodall Ave. A2
Wrea La. A2
York Pl. A4/B4

Sheffield

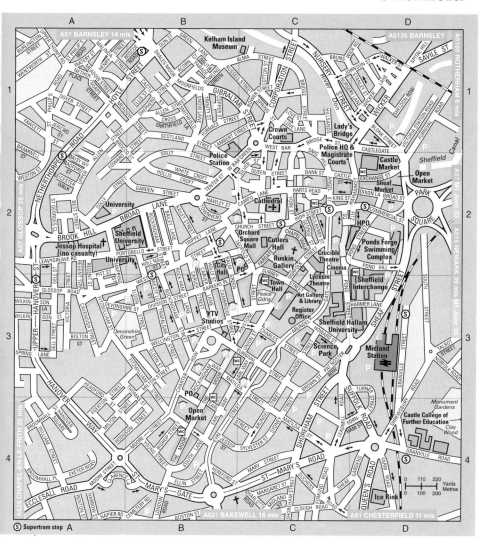

Acorn St. B1
Allen St. B1
Alma St. C1
Angel St. C2
Arundel Gate C2/C3
Arundel St. C3/C4
Bailey La. B2
Bailey St. B2
Balm Gn. B2
Bank St. C2
Barkers Pl. B3
Best St. A2
Bishop St. B4
Blonk St. D1

Bolton St. A3
Boston St. B4
Bower St. C1
Bowling Gn. B1
Bramwell St. A1/A2
Bridge St. C1
Broad La. A2/B2
Broad St. D2
Brocco St. A1/B2
Broomhall Pl. A4
Broomhall St. A4
Brown St. C3
Brunswick Rd. C1
Burlington St. A1

Cambridge St. B3
Campo La. C2
Carver La. B2/B3
Carver St. B2/B3
Castle Gate D1
Castle St. B1
Castle St. C2
Cavendish St. A3
Cemetery Rd. B4
Chapel Walk C2
Charles St. C3
Charlotte Rd. C4
Charter Row B3
Church St. C2

Clarence La. A4
Clough Rd. C4
Commercial St. D2
Corporation St. C1
Cotton St. C1
Cross Smithfield B1
Daisy Way A2
Devonshire St. A3
Division St. B3
Dixon La. D2
Dover St. A1
Duchess Rd. C4
Dun St. B1
Earl St. B4/C4

Earl Way B4/C3
Ecclesall Rd. A4
Edmund Rd. C4
Edward St. A2/B1
Egerton St. A3/A4
Eldon St. B3
Ellin St. B4
Ellis St. B1
Exchange St. D2
Exeter Rd. A4
Eyre St. B4
Fargate C2
Farm Rd. D4
Fawcett St. A1

Fitzalan Sq. C2/D2
Fitzwilliam St. A3/B3
Fornham St. C4/D4
Furnace St. B1
Furnival Rd. D1
Furnival St. B3/C3
Garden St. B2
Gell St. A3
George St. C2
Gibralter St. B1/C1
Glossop Rd. A3
Granville Rd. D4
Granville St. D3
Green La. B1

Hanover Sq. A4
Hanover Way A3/A4
Harmer La. D3
Harrow St. A4
Harts Head C2
Hawley St. B2
Headford St. A3/A4
Henry St. A1
Hereford St. B4
High St. C2
Hillsands C1
Hodgson St. A4/B4
Holland St. B2
Hollis Croft B2

Index continued on page 66

65

Sheffield

Continued from page 65

Lambert St. B1/C1	Midland St. C4	Pitt St. A2/3	Russell St. B1/C1
Leadmill Rd. C4	Milton St. A4/B3	Pond Hill D2	St. George's Cl. A2
Leavygreave Rd. A2	Moore St. A4/B4	Pond St. C3/D2	St. Marys Gate B4
Leicester Walk A2	Mulberry St. C2	Portobello St. A2/B2	St. Mary's Rd. C4
Leopold St. C2	Napier Rd. A4	Queen St. C2	St. Philip's Rd. A1
London Rd. B4	Nether Pl. A1	Queen's Rd. D4	Savile St. D1
Love La. C1	Netherthorpe Rd. A1/A2	Radford St. A2	Scotland St. B1
Love St. C1	Norfolk Rd. D3	Regent St. A2/A3	Shales Moor B1
Moorfields B1	Norfolk St. C3	Regent Ter. A2/A3	Sheaf Gdns. C4/D4
Malinda St. A1	Nursery La. C1/D1	Renton St. A4	Sheaf St. D2/D3
Mapping St. A2	Nursery St. C1	Rockingham La. B3	Sheldon Row D1
Mary St. C4	Park Sq. D2	Rockingham St. B2/B3	Shepherd St. B1
Matilda St. B3/C4	Paternoster Row C3	Rockingham Way B3	Shoreham St. C4
Meadow St. A1	Pinstone St. C3	Roscoe Rd. B1	Shrewsbury Rd. D3/D4

Snig Hill C2	Thomas St. B3/B4	West Bar Gn. B2/C2
Snow La. B1	Townhead St. B2	West St. B2/B3
Solly St. A2/B2	Trafalgar St. B3	Westfield St. B3
South La. B4	Trinity St. B1	Weston St. A2
South Pde. B1	Trippet La. B2	White Croft B2
South St. D2/D3	Turner St. D3	Wicker La. D1
Spring La. A3	Upper Alien St. A1/A2	Wicker Spital Hill D1
Spring St. C1	Upper Hanover St. A3	Wilkinson La. A3
Stanley St. D1	Upper Thorpe Rd. A1	Wilkinson St. A3
Suffolk Rd. C3/D4	Victoria St. A3	William St. A4
Surrey St. C2/C3	Victoria Station Rd. D1	Young St. B4
Sydney St. C4	Walker St. D1	
Sylvester St. C4	Watery St. A1	
Talbot St. D3	Wellington St. B3	
Silver St. C2	Tenter St. B2	Wentworth St. A1
Smithfield La. B1	The Moor B3/B4	West Bar C1

On the Motorway

- If you have vehicle problems, try to drive to the next emergency telephone. If you have to walk, directional arrows on marker posts point to the nearest telephone.

- Switch on your hazard warning lights, and keep your sidelights on if it is dark or visibility is poor.

- Walk on the inside of the hard shoulder, and when you reach the phone, stand behind it facing on-coming traffic.

- Return to your car and lock all the doors except the passenger door. Stay on the embankment unless you feel there is an obvious danger.

- If an unidentified vehicle draws up, get back in the car and lock the door.

- If anyone offers to help, ask them to contact the appropriate emergency service, rather than assist personally.

- If you see another driver in difficulty, drive on and report it by telephone as soon as possible.

- Never pick up hitch-hikers.

Shrewsbury

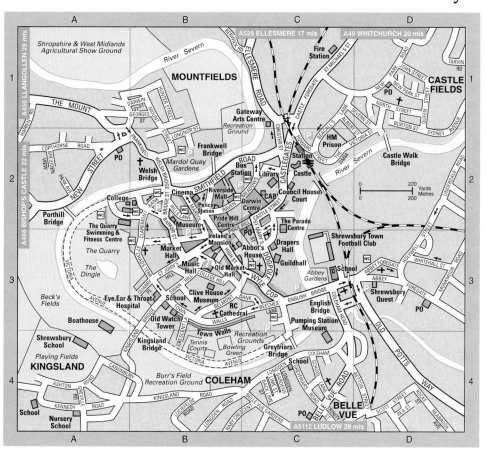

Abbey Foregate D3	Bridge St. B2	Dogpole C3	Kennedy Rd. A4	New Park St. D1	School La. C4	The Mount A1
Albert St. C1	Burton St. D1	Ellesmere Rd. C1	Kingsland Br. A4/B3	New St. A2	Scott St. D4	Town Walls B3
Ashton Rd. A4	Canonbury A4	English Br. C3	Kingsland Rd. B4	North St. D1	Severn St. D1	Trinity St. C4
Back Lime St. C4	Castle Foregate C1	Frankwell B2	Lime St. C4	Old Potts Way D4	Smithfield Rd. B2	Underdale Rd. D2
Barker St. B2/3	Castle St. C2	Greville Rd. A4	Longden Coleham C4	Park Ave. A2	St Chads Ter. B3	Victoria Ave. A3/B4
Beacall's La. C1/2	Castlegates C2	Greyfriars Rd. C4	Longden Gardens C4	Pride Hill B3/C2	St Georges St. B1	Victoria St. D2
Beeches La. C3	Chester St. C2	Hafren Rd. A1	Longden Rd. B4	Quarry Place B3	St John's Hill B3	Welsh Br. B2
Belle Vue Gardens C4	Claremont Bank B2	High St. B3	Longnor St. B2	Queen St. D1	St Mary's St. C2/3	Whitehall St. D3
Belle Vue Rd. C4	Coleham Head C3	Hills La. B2	Luciefelde Rd. B4	Raby Cres. B4	St Michael's St. C1	Wyle Cop.C3
Belmont Bank B3/C3	College Hil B3	Holywell St. D3	Mardol B2	Raven Meadows B2/C2	Swan Hil B3	
Berwick Rd. B1	Copthorne Rd. A2	Howard St. C2	Monkmoor Rd. D3	Rea St. D4	Sydney Ave. D2	
Betton St. D4	Crescent La. B3/4	Hunter St. B1	Mount St. B1	Reabrook St. D4	Tarvin Rd. D1	
Breidden View A2	Darwin St. B1	John St. D1	New Park Rd. D1	Rocke St. D4	The Dana C2	

Seatbelts save lives

It is the driver's responsibility to ensure that passengers under the age of 14 are wearing seatbelts. Children under the age of 11 should wear an appropriate child restraint. Remember, in the event of an accident at 30mph, a child in a rear seat could be thrown forward with the force equivalent to the weight of a baby elephant.

Southampton

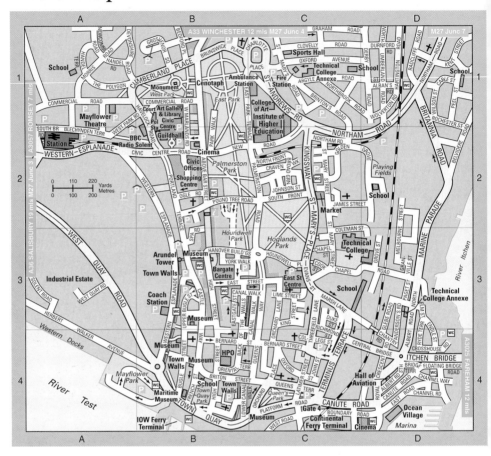

Above Bar St. B2
Albert Rd. North D3/D4
Albert Rd. South D4
Anderson's Rd. D3/D4
Argyle Rd. C1
Back of the Walls B3/B4
Bedford Pl. B1
Belvidere Rd. D2
Bernard St. B4/C4
Blechynden Ter. A2
Boundary Rd. C4
Bridge Ter. D4
Brinton's Rd. C1
Britannia Rd. D1/D2
Briton St. B4
Broad Gn. C2
Brunswick Pl. B1
Bugle St. B4
Cable St. D1

Canal Walk B3/C3
Canute Rd. C4/D4
Castle Way B3
Central Bridge D4
Channel Rd. D4
Channel Way D4
Chantry Rd. D4
Chapel Rd. C3/D3
Chapel St. C3
Civic Centre Rd. B2
Clovelly Rd. C1
Coleman St. C2/C3
College St. C4
Commercial Rd. A1/B1
Cook St. C3
Craven Walk C2
Crosshouse Rd. C4
Cumberland Pl. B1
Derby Rd. D1

Devonshire Rd. A1
Duke St. C3
Durnford Rd. D1
East Park Ter. B1
East Rd. D4
East St. B3/C3
Eastgate St. B3
Elm St. D3
Endle St. D3/D4
Evans St. C3
Floating Bridge Rd. D4
French St. B4
Glebe Rd. D3
Golden Grove C2/D2
Graham Rd. C1
Granville St. D3
Grosvenor Sq. B1
Grove St. B3
Handel Rd. A1

Handel Ter. A1
Hanover Buildings B3
Hartington Rd. D1
Havelock Rd. B1
Herbert Walker Ave. A3/A4
High St. B3/B4
Houndwell Pl. C3
Itchen Bridge D4
James St. C2
John St. C4
Johnson St. C2
Kent St. D1
King St. C3
Kingsway C2
Latimer St. C4
Lime St. C3
Lwr Canal Walk B4
Marine Pde. D2/D3

Marsh La. C3
Melbourne St. D2/D3
Morris Rd. A1
New Rd. B2/C2
Newcombe Rd. A1
North Front C2
Northam Rd. C2/D1
Northbrook Rd. C1
Northumberland Rd. D1
Ogle Rd. B2
Orchard La. C3
Orchard Pl. C4
Oriental Ter. B4
Oxford Ave. C1
Oxford St. C4
Page St. D3
Palmerston Rd. C2
Park Walk B2

Peel St. D1
Platform Rd. C4
Portland Ter. B2
Pound Tree Rd. B2
Queens Ter. C4
Queens Way C3/C4
Radcliffe Rd. D1
Richmond St. C4
Rochester St. D1
Royal Crescent Rd. D4
Ryde Ter. D4
Solent Rd. A3
South Bridge Rd. A2
South Front C2
Spa Rd. B3
St. Alban's Rd. D1
St. Andrews Rd. C4
St. Mary St. C2/C3
St. Mary's Pl. C2

St. Mary's Rd. C1
Terminus Ter. C4
The Polygon A1
Threefield La. C3
Town Quay B4
Upper Bugle St. B3
West Marlands Rd. B1
West Park Rd. A2
West Quay Rd. A3
West Rd. C4
Western Esplanade A2/B4
Wilson St. D1
Wolverton Rd. D1
York Walk B3

68

Stockport

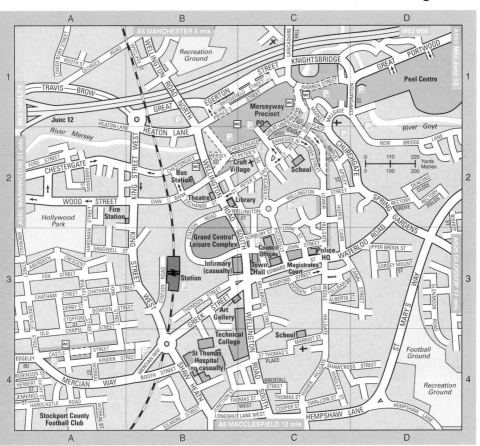

Aberdeen Cres. A3
Alberta St. C3
Apsley St. C2
Bamford St. C3
Bishop St. D2
Booth St. B4
Bosden Fold C3
Bowden St. A3
Brentall St. C4
Bridgefield St. B1
Bulkeley St. A3
Canal St. D3
Castle St. A4
Chatham St. A3/B3
Chestergate A2/C2

Churchgate C2
Cooper St. C4
Corporation St. D1
Daw Bank B2
Deacons Cl. D2
Derby St. A3
Edgeley Rd. A4
Edward St. C3
Exchange St. B2
Ford St. A2
Fox St. A3
Georges Rd. A1
Gilmore St. B4
Glenmoor Rd. D3
Gorsey Mount St. D3

Gradwell St. A3
Great Egerton St.
  B1/C1
Great Portwood.D1
Great Underbank.C2
Greek St. B3
Grenville St. A3/A4
Hardcastle Rd. A4
Hardman St. A2/A3
Harvey St. C2
Heaton La. A1/B2
Hempshaw La. C4/D4
Herbert St. A4
High Bankside.C2
High St. C2

Higher Hillgate.C4
Hindley St. C4
Hopes Carr C2
Jennings St. A4
John St. C3
Junction St. B4
Kinder St. A4
King Street West
  B2/B3
Knightsbridge C1
Lancashire Hill C1
Little Underbank C1
Longshut Lane West B4
Lowe St. C3
Lower Bury St. A1

Lower Hillgate C2
Market Pl. C1
Marriot St. C4
Mercian Way. A4/B4
Mersey Sq. B2
Middle Hillgate C3
Millbrook St. C3
Millgate C1
New Bridge La. D2
Norbury St. C3
Old Chapel St. A4
Piccadilly C2/C3
Prince's St. B1
Rectory Fields D2
Rectory Grove D2

Robinson St. A4
Rooth St. A1
Shaw Heath B4
Shawcross St. C4
Spring Gdns. D2
St Mary's Way.D3
St Peter's Gate.C2
St Peter's Sq. C2
St Thomas's Pl. C4
Station Rd. B3
Stopford St. A3
Swallow St. C4
Thomas St. C4
Thomas Street West
  B4

Thomson St. B3
Tollbar St. C3
Travis Brow A1
Upper Brook St. D3
Warren St. C1
Waterloo Rd. C3
Wellington Rd. North
  B1
Wellington Rd. South
  B2/C4
Wellington St. B2/C2
Wood St. A2
Worral St. A4
Wycliffe St. A1
York St. A3

Stoke-on-Trent

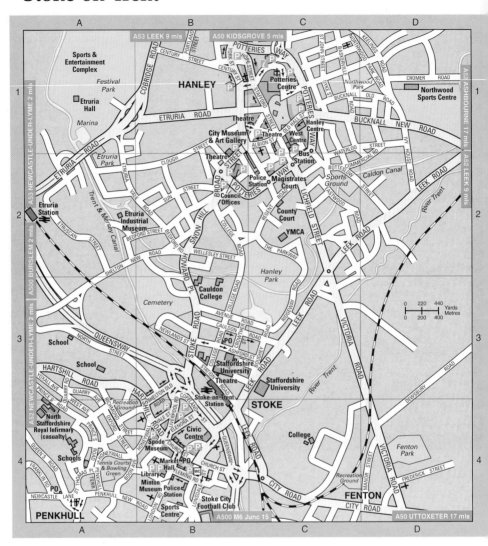

Albion St. C1	Century St. B1	Dewsbury Rd. D3	Hope St. B1/C1	Newlamds St. B3	Quarry Rd. A3	Stafford St. C1
Ashford St. B3	Church St. B4	Dyke St. C1	Howard Pl. B2	North St. A3	Quarry Ave A3	Station Rd. B3
Avenue Rd. B3	City Rd. C4/D4	Eastwood Rd. C2	Ivy House Rd. D1/D2	Northwood Park Rd.	Queen's Rd. A4	Stoke Rd. B3
Baskerville Rd. C1	Clough St. B2	Elenora St. B4	Keelings Rd. D1	C1/D1	Queensway A3/B4	Sun St. B2
Bedford Rd. A2	College Rd. B2	Etruria Rd. A2/B2	Leek Rd. D2	Old Hall St. C1	Regent Rd. C2	The Parkway C2
Boon Ave. A4	College Rd. B3	Etruria Rd. A2/B2	Leek Rd. B4/C3/D2	Oxford St. A4	Richmond St. A4	Vale St. B4
Botteslow St. C2/D2	Commercial Rd. C2/D2	Etruscan St. A2	Lichfield St. C2	Penkhull New Rd. A4	Ringway Rd. B3	Victoria St. C3/D4
Boughey Rd. C3	Copeland St. B4	Fleming Rd. B4	Liverpool Rd. B4	Penkhull Ter. A4	Shelton New Rd. A2	Voxall Ave A3
Brd. St. B2	Corbridge Rd. B1	Franklin La. A4	London Rd. B4	Portland St. B1	Shelton Old Rd. B3	Waterloo St. C1/D1
Bucknall Old Rd. C1/D1	Cromer Rd. D1	Frederick St. D4	Lonsdale St. B4	Potteries Way B2/C2	Snow Hill B2	Wellesley St. B2
Bucknall New Rd. D1	Crowther St. B3	Hartshill Rd. A3/B4	Manor St. D4	Potteries Way B1/C1	St Johns Streeet C1	West Ave A4
Cauldon Rd. B3		Honeywall A4/B4	Newcastle La. A4	Prince's Rd. A3/A4	St Thomas Pl. A4	York St. B1

70

Stratford-upon-Avon

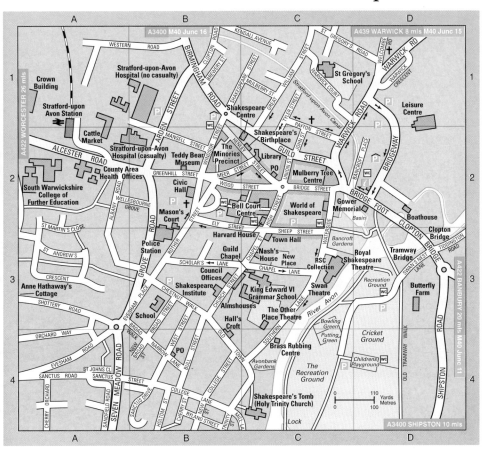

Albany Rd. A2
Alcester Rd. A2
Arden St. B1/B2
Bancroft Pl. D2
Bell Court B2
Birmingham Rd. B1
Brewery St. B1
Bridge Foot D2
Bridge St. C2
Bridgeway D2
Broad St. B3
Broad Walk B4

Bull St. B4
Chapel La. C3
Chapel St. C3
Cherry Orchard A4
Cherry St. B4
Chestnut Walk B3
Church St. B3
Clopton Bridge D2/D3
Clopton Rd. B1
College La. B4
College St. B4
Ely St. B2

Evesham Pl. B3
Evesham Rd. A4
Great William St. C1
Greenhill St. B2
Grove Rd. B3
Guild St. C2
Henley St. B2/C2
High St. C2
Holtom St. B4
John St. C2
Kendall Ave. C1
Mansell St. B2

Meer St. B2
Mill La. B4
Mulberry St. C1
Narrow La. B4
New Broad St. B4
New St. B4
Old Town B4
Old Tramway Walk D4
Orchard Way A4
Payton St. C2
Rother St. B3
Ryland St. B4

Sanctus Dr. B4
Sanctus Rd. A4
Sanctus St. A4
Sandfield Rd. A4
Scholar's La. B3
Seven Meadow Rd. A4
Shakespeare St. B1
Sheep St. C3
Shipston Rd. D4
Southern La. C3/C4
St. Andrew's Cres. A3

St. Gregory's Rd. C1
St. Johns Cl. A4
St. Martin's Cl. A2
Swan's Nest La. D3
Tiddington Rd. D3
Trinity St. B4
Tyler St. C1
Union St. C2
Warwick Court C1
Warwick Cres. D1
Warwick Rd. C2/D1
Waterside C2/C3

Welcombe Rd. D1
Wellesbourne Grove A2
West St. B4
Western Rd. A1
Windsor St. B2
Wood St. B2

Seatbelts save lives

It is the driver's responsibility to ensure that passengers under the age of 14 are wearing seatbelts. Children under the age of 11 should wear an appropriate child restraint. Remember, in the event of an accident at 30mph, a child in a rear seat could be thrown forward with the force equivalent to the weight of a baby elephant.

Swansea

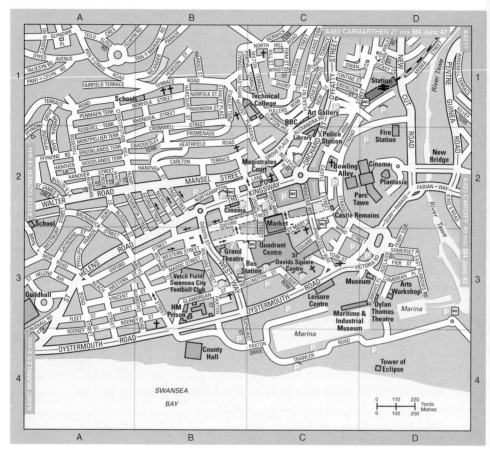

Adelaide St. D3
Albert Row C3
Alexandra Rd. C1
Argyle St. B3
Bathurst St. B3/B4
Beach St. A3
Bellevue Way C2
Berwick Ter. C1
Bond St. A3
Brooklands Ter. A2
Brunswick St. A2
Bryn-Syfi Ter. B1
Bryn-y-Mor Rd. A3
Bullin's La. A2
Burman St. A2
Burrows Pl. D3
Burrows Rd. B3
Cadfan Rd. A1
Cambrian Pl. D3
Carlton Ter. B2

Castle St. C2
Catherine St. A3
Chaddesley Ter. B2
Clifton Hill. C1
Constitution Hill A1/A2
Craig Ter. C1
Crole St. A2
Cromwell St. B2
Dilwyn St. B3
Duke St. A2
Dyfatty St. C1
Dyfed Ave. A1
East Burrows Rd. D3
Ebenezer St. C1
Elfed Rd. A1
Evans Ter. C1
Fabian Way. D2
Fairfield Ter. A1
Ferry Side D3
Ffynone Cl. A2

Ffynone Dr. A2
Ffynone Rd. A2
Firm St. C1
Fleet St. A3
Fullers Row C1
George St. B2
Glamorgan St. B3
Glyndwr Pl. A1
Grove Pl. C2
Guildhall Rd Sth. A3
Hanover La. A2
Hanover St. A2/B2
Harries St. B1
Heathfield Rd. B2
Henrietta St. A2
Hewson St. B1
High St. C1
Hill St. C1
Hump St. C2
Islwyn Rd. A1

Jockey St. D1
John St. D1
Jones Ter. C1
Kilvey Ter. D1
King's Rd. D2
Madoc St. B3
Mansel St. B2
Milton Ter. C1
Montpellier Ter. A2
Morfa St. D1
Mount Pleasant B1
New Cut Rd. D1/D2
New St. C1
Nicander Pde. B1
Nicholl St. B2
Norfolk St. B1
North Hill Rd. C1
Northampton La. B2
Orchard St. C2
Oxford St. A3/B2

Oystermouth Rd. A4/C3
Page St. B2
Pant-y-Celyn Rd. A1
Paxton Dr. C4
Paxton St. B3
Pen-y-Craig Rd. A1
Penmaen Ter. A1
Pentre Guinea Rd. D1/D2
Phillips Parade A3
Pier St. D3
Pleasant View Ter. C1
Portia Ter. B1
Portland St. C2
Prince of Wales Rd. D1
Princess Way C2/C3
Quay Parade D2
Rhianfa La. A1/A2
Rhondda St. B1
Richard St. B3

Rodney St. A3/A4
Rosehill A2
Rosehill Ter. A2
Russell St. A2/A3
St. Davids Sq. C3
St. Helens Ave. A3
St. Helens Rd. A3
St. James's Cres. A2
St. Mary's Sq. C3
Stanley Pl. B1
Stanley Ter. B1
Strand C2
Swan St. C1
Taliesyn Rd. A1
Tan-y-Marian Rd. B1
Teilo Cres. A1
Terrace Rd. A1/B1
The Kingsway B2/C2

Tontine St. C1
Trawler Rd. C4
Union St. C2
Victoria Rd. D3
Vincent St. A3
Walter Rd. A2
Watkin St. C1
Wellington St. C3
West Way B3
Westbury St. A3
Western St. A3/B3
White St. A2
William St. B3
Wind St. C3
Windmill Ter. D1
Winston St. C1
Woodlands Ter. A2
York St. C3

Telford

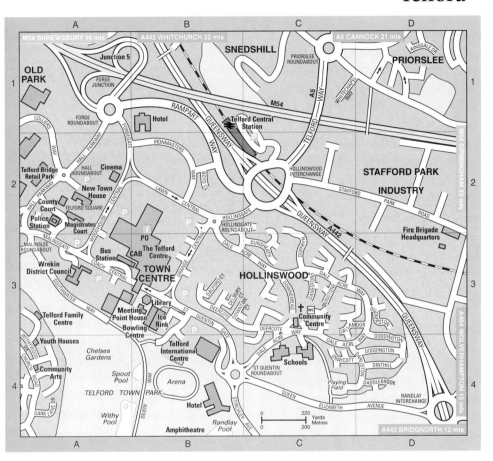

Ainsdale Dr. D1	Dalford Court B3	Dinthill D4	Dunsheath C3	Lawn Central B2	Southwater Way A3	Whitechapel Way C1
Boyd Cl. B2	Dallamoor C3	Doddington D4	Dunstone C3	Malinsgate A3	St Quentin Gate B3	Withywood Dr. A4
Church Rd. A4	Danesford C3	Downemead C3	Forgegate A1/2	Queen Elizabeth Ave.	Stafford Park Road	Woodhouse Central
Coach Central A3	Dark Lane Dr. A4	Downton Court B3	Grange Central B3	C4	C2/D2	A2
Colliers Way A1/2	Darliston D4	Draycott C4	Hall Parkway A2	Queensway B1/D3	Stirchley Ave. B4	
Daddlebrook D4	Deercote B3/C3	Dudmaston D3	Hollinsgate B2	Rampart Way B1	Telford Sq. A2	
Dale Acre Way B3/C4	Delbury Court B3	Duffryn C3	Ironmasters Way B2	Silkin Way B4	Telford Way C1/2	

What to carry in your car

Don't be at a loss if you break down or are involved in an accident.
The following items can be easily stored in your vehicle and will prove useful - torch, hazard
warning triangle, jump leads, tow rope, first aid kit, and blanket. In winter, always carry warm
clothing and a pair of wellington boots.

Torquay

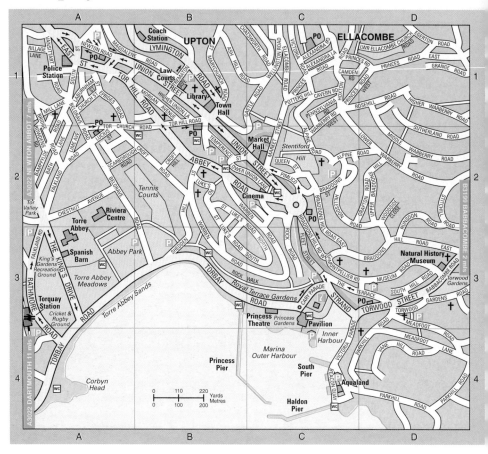

Abbey Rd. B2
Alexandra La. C1
Alexandra Rd. C1
Alpine Rd. C2
Ash Hill Rd. B1
Babbacombe Rd. D3
Bampfylde Rd. A2
Bath La. A2
Beacon Quay D4
Belgrave Rd. A1/A2
Braddons Hill Road
East C2
Braddons Hill Road
West C3
Braddons St. C2
Bridge Rd. A1

Camden Rd. C1
Cary Pde. C3
Castle Rd. C1
Cavern Rd. C1
Chatsworth Rd. C1
Chestnut Ave. A2
Church St. A1
Croft Hill B2
Croft Rd. B2
East St. A1
Egerton Rd. D1
Ellacombe Rd. C1
Falkland Rd. A2
Fleet St. C3
Grafton Rd. D2
Grange Rd. D1

Higher Union La. B1
Higher Warberry Rd.
D1
Hillesdon Rd. C2
Hoxton Rd. C1
Hunsdon Rd. D2
Laburnham St. A1
Lime Ave. A2
Lower Ellacombe
Church Rd. D1
Lower Union Ave. B2
Lower Warberry Rd.
D2
Lucius St. A2
Lymington Rd. B1
Magdalene Rd. A1

Market St. C2
Meadfoot La. D4
Meadfoot Rd. D3
Middle Warberry Rd.
D2
Mill La. A1
Montpellier Rd. C3
Morgan Ave. B1
Museum Rd. D3
Newton Rd. A1
Parkhill Rd. D4
Pennsylvania Rd. C1
Pimlico.C2
Potters Hill.C1
Princes Road East D1
Princes Road West C1

Princes Rd. C1/D1
Queen St. C2
Rathmore Rd. A3
Rillage La. A1
Rock Rd. C3
Rock Walk B3
Rosehill Rd. D1
Rowdens Rd. A2
Scarborough Rd. A2
Shedden Hill B3
South Hill Rd. D3
South St. A1
St Efrides Rd. A1
St Luke's Road North
B2
St Luke's Road Sth B2

St Luke's Rd. B2
St Marychurch Rd. B1
Stitchill Rd. D2
Strand C3
Sutherland Rd. D2
Temperence St. B2
The King's Dr. A3
The Terrace D3
Tor Church Rd. A2
Tor Hill Rd. A1/B1
Torbay Rd. A4/B3
Torwood Gardens Rd.
D3
Torwood St. D3
Trematon Ave. B1
Union St. B1

Upper Braddons Hill
D2
Vane Hill Rd. D4
Vansittart Rd. A1
Victoria Pde. C4
Victoria Rd. C1
Warberry Road West
C1
Warren Rd. B3/C2
Wellington Rd. C1
Woodside Close D2

Watford

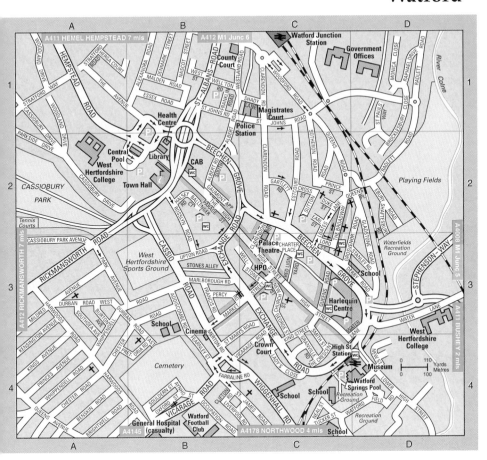

Addiscombe Rd. B3	Chester Rd. A4/B3	Fearnley St. B4	Lady's Cl. C4	Park Ave. A3	Smith St. C3	The Parade B2
Albert Road South B2	Church St. C3	Francis Rd. B3	Liverpool Rd. B4	Parkside Dr. A2	Sotheron Rd. C2	Tucker St. C4
Albert Rd. B2	Clarendon Rd. C1/C3	Franklin Rd. B1	Loates La. C2	Percy Rd. B3	Souldern St. B4	Upton Rd. B3
Alexandra Rd. B1	Clifton Rd. B4	Gartlett Rd. C2	Lord St. C3	Pretoria Rd. B4	Southsea Ave. A3	Vicarage Rd. B4/C4
Aynho St. B4	Cross St. C2	Gaumont Approach B2	Lower High St. D4	Prince St. C2	St Albans Rd. B1	Water La. D3
Ballenger Court B2	Denmark St. B1	George St. C3	Malden Rd. B1	Princes Ave. A4	St James Rd. C4	Watford Field Rd. D4
Beechen Grove B2/C3	Derby Rd. D3	Gladstone Rd. D2/3	Market St. B3	Queens Ave. A4	St Johns Rd. B1/C1	Wellington Rd. B1
Benskin Rd. A4	Duke St. C2	Granville Rd. C4	Marlborough Rd. B3	Queens Pl. D2	St Marys Rd. B4	Wellstones C3
Brightwell Rd. A4	Durban Road East	Grosvenor Rd. C3	Merton Rd. B4	Queens Rd. C2	St Pauls Way D1	West St. B1
Brocklesbury Close D1	A3/B3	Halsey Rd. B2	Mildred Ave. A3	Queens Rd. C3	Stanley Rd. D3	Westland Rd. B1
Burton Ave. A3	Durban Road West A3	Harwoods Rd. A3/A4	Monica Cl. D1	Radlett Rd. D1/D2	Stones Alley B3	Whippendell Rd. A4/B3
Cassio Rd. B3	Earl St. C2	Hempstead Rd. A1	Nascot St. B1	Raphael Dr. D1	Stratford Rd. A1	Wiggenhall Rd. C4
Cassiobury Drive	Ebury Rd. D2	Herga Court A1	Neal St. C4	Red Lion Yard.C3	Stratford Way A1	Woodford Rd. C1
A1/A2	Essex Rd. B1	High St. B2/C3	New St. C3	Rickmansworth Rd. A3	Sutton Rd. C2	Woodland Dr. A1
Cassiobury Park Ave.	Estcourt Rd. C2	Kensington Ave. A4	New St. D4	Rosslyn Rd. B2	The Ave. A1	
A3	Exchange Rd. B3/C4	King St. C4	Occupation Rd. B4	Shady La. C1	The Broadway C2	
Charter Pl. C3	Farraline Rd. B4	Kings Ave. A4	Oxford St. B4	Shaftesbury Rd. D2	The Crescent C4	

Winchester

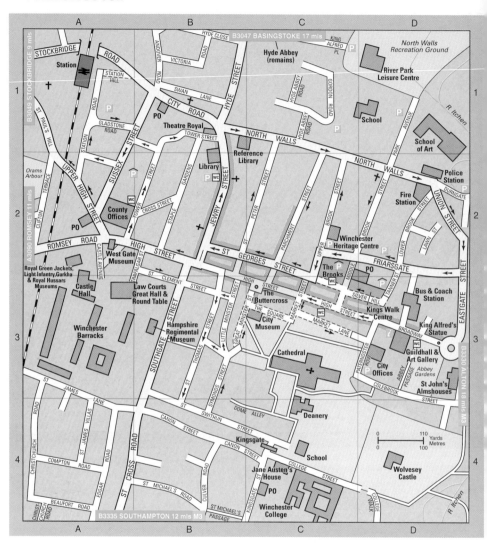

Abbey Passage D3
Andover Rd. B1
Beaufort Rd. A4
Broadway D3
Canon St. B4/C4
Castle Ave. A2
Christchurch Rd. A4
City Rd. B1
Clifton Ter. A2
Colebrook St. D3

College St. C4
College Walk D4
Compton Rd .A4
Cross St. B2
Culver Rd. B4
Dome Alley B4/C4
Durngate D2
Eastgate St. D3
Edgar Rd. A4
Friarsgate D2

Gladstone Rd. A1
Gordon Rd. C1
Great Minster St. B3
High St. B2/C3
Hyde Abbey Rd. C1
Hyde Cl. B1
Hyde St. B1
Jewry St. B2
King Alfred Pl. C1
Kingsgate St. C4

Lawn St. D2
Little Minster St. B3
Lower Brook St. D2
Market La. C3
Market St. C3
Middle Brook St.
  C2/D2
North Walls C1/D2
Parchment St. C2
Park Ave. D1

Romsey Rd. A2
Silver Hill D3
Southgate St. B3
St. Clement St. B3
St. Cross Rd. A4
St. Georges St. B2/C2
St. James La. A3
St. James Villas A4
St. Michael's Passage
  B4

St. Michael's Rd. B4
St. Paul's Hill A1
St. Peter St. C2
St. Swithun St. B4
St. Thomas St. B3
Staple Gdns. B2
Station Hill A1
Station Rd. A1
Stockbridge Rd. A1
Sussex St. A2

Swan La. B1
Symonds St. B3
Tanner St. D3
The Square C3
Tower St. B1/B2
Trafalgar St. B2
Union St. D2
Upper Brook St. C2
Upper High St. A2
Victoria Rd. B1

Wolverhampton

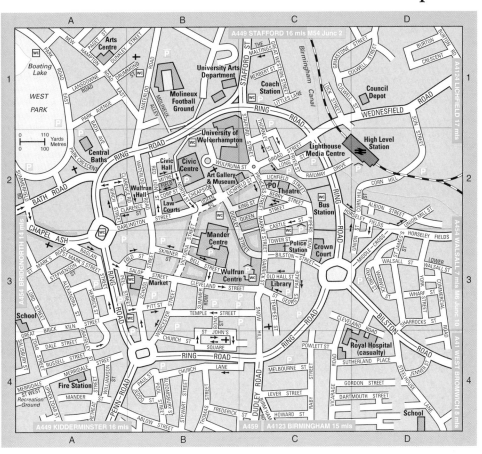

Ablow St. B4	Church St. B4	Garrick St. C3	Lower Walsall St. D3	Peel St. A3	Skinner St. B3	Tower St. C3
Albion St. D2	Clarence Rd. A2	Gordon St. D4	Mander St. A4	Penn Rd. A4	Snow Hill C3	Union Mill St. D2
Alexandra St. A3	Clarence St. B2	Graiseley St. A4	Market St. C2	Pipers Row C2	St Georges Parade C3	Union St. D3
Bath Ave. A1	Cleveland Rd. C3	Great Brick Kiln St. A3	Melbourne St. C4	Pitt St. B3	St James's St. D3	Upper Zoar St. A4
Bath Rd. A2	Cleveland St. B3	Great Western St. C1	Merridale St. A4	Pool St. B4	St John's Sq. B4	Vicarage Rd. C4
Bell St. B3	Commercial Rd. D3	Grimstone St. C1	Merridale Street West	Powlett St. C4	St Mark's Rd. A3	Victoria St. B3
Berry St. C2	Corn Hill D2	Herbert St. C1	A4	Princess St. C2	St Mark's St. A3	Walsall St. D3
Bilston Rd. D3	Corn Hill St. D2	Herrick St. A3	Middle Cross D3	Queen Sq. B2	Stafford St. B1/C2	Warwick St. D3
Bilston St. C3	Corporation St. B2	Horseley Fields D2	Mitre Field B2	Queen St. C2	Steelhouse La. D4	Waterloo Rd. B1/B2
Birch St. A2	Culwell St. C1	Howard St. C4	Molineux Alley B1	Raby St. C4	Stephenson St. A3	Wednesfield Rd. D1
Birmingham Rd. C4	Dale St. A4	Jeddo St. B4	New Hampton Road	Raglan St. A3	Stewart St. B4	Wharf St. D3
Bloomsbury St. B4	Darlington St. B2	Jenner St. D4	East A1	Railway Dr. C2	Summer Row B3	Williamson St. A4
Bond St. B3	Dartmouth St. D4	King St. C2	North St. B2	Red Lion St. B2	Summerfield Rd. A2	Worcester St. B3
Broad St. C2	Drummond St. A1	Lansdowne Rd. A1	Old Hall St. C3	Retreat St. A4	Sun St. D1	Wulfruna St. B2
Burton Cres. D1	Dudley Rd. C4	Lever St. C4	Oxford St. D3	Ring Rd. A2/C4	Sutherland Pl. D4	York St. D3
Burton Rd. D1	Dudley St. B2	Lichfield St. B2/C2	Paget St. A1	Russell St. A4	Tempest St. C3	Zoar St. A4
Castle St. C2	Dunkley St. A1	Littles La. C1	Park Ave. A1	Salisbury St. A4	Temple St. B3	
Chapel Ash A3	Fold St. B3	Lock St. C1	Park Cres. A2	Salop St. B3	The Maltings C1	
Cheapside B2	Frederick St. B4	Long St. C2	Park Road East A1	School St. B3	Thomas St. B4	
Church La. B4	Fryer St. C2	Lord St. A3	Paul St. B4	Sharrocks St. D3	Thornley St. C2	

York

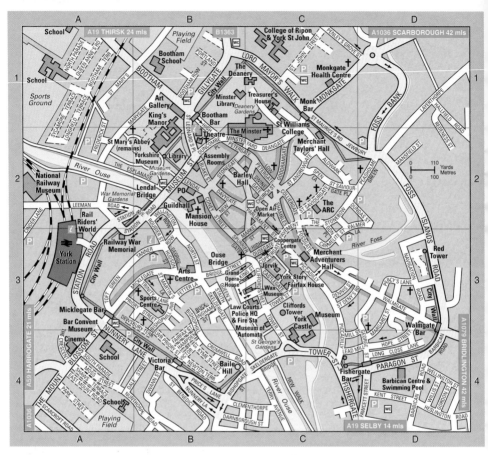

Aldwark C2
Barbican Rd. D4
Bishopgate St. B4
Bishophill Junction B3
Blake St. B2
Blossom St. A4
Bootham B1
Bootham Row B1
Bootham Ter. A1
Bridge St. B3
Buckingham St. B3
Carmelite St. C3
Castlegate C3
Church St. C2
Cinder La. A2
Clementhorpe B4/C4
Clifford St. C3
Colliergate C2
Coney St. B2

Coppergate C3
Cromwell Rd. B4
Dale St. A4/B4
Darnborough St. B4/C4
Davygate B2
Deangate C2
Dennis St. C3
Dewsbury Ter. A3/B4
Duncombe Pl. B2
Dundas St. C2/D2
East Mount Rd. A4
Fairfax St. B4
Fawcett St. D4
Fetter La. B3
Fishergate C4
Foss Bank D1
Foss Islands Rd. D2/D3
Fossgate C3

Frederick St. A2
Garden Pl. C3
George St. C3/D4
George Hudson St. B3
Gillygate B1
Goodramgate C2
Gordon St. D4
Hallfield Rd. D1
Hampden St. B4
Heslington Rd. D4
High Ousegate C3
High Petergate B1/B2
Hope St. D4
Jewbury C2/D2
Kent St. D4
King St. B3
Kyme St. B4
Layerthorpe D1
Lead Mill St. C4

Leeman Rd. A2
Lendal B2
Long Close La. D4
Longfield Ter. A1/A2
Lord Mayor's Walk C1
Low Petergate C2
Lower Priory St. B4
Mansfield St. D2
Margaret St. D3/D4
Market St. B3/C2
Marygate A2/B1
Micklegate A3/B3
Mill St. C4
Minster Yard B2/C2
Monkgate C1
Moss St. A4
Museum St. B2
Navigation Rd. D3
New St. B2

Newton Ter. B4
North Pde. A1
North St. B3
Nunnery A4/B4
Nunthorpe Rd. A4/B4
Palmer La. C2
Paragon St. D4
Park St. A4
Parliament St. C2/C3
Pavement C3
Penley's Grove St. C1
Percy's La. D3
Piccadilly C3
Portland St. B1
Price's La. B4
Priory St. A3/B3
Queen Anne's Rd. A1
Queen's Staith B3
Redeness St. D1/D2

Rougier St. B2/B3
St. Andrewgate C2
St. Benedict Rd. B4
St. Deny's Rd. C3
St. John St. C1
St. Leonard's Pl. B1/B2
St. Martin's La. B3
St. Maurice's Rd. C1/C2
St. Mary's A1
St. Saviourgate C2
St. Saviourgate Pl. C2
Scarcroft Rd. A4
Shaws Ter. A4
Skelder Gate Bridge C4
Skeldergate B3/B4
South Pde. A4
Spen La. C2
Spurrier Gate B3
Station Ave. A2

Station Rd. A3
Stonegate B2
Swann St. B4
Swine Gate C2
Sycamore Ter. A1
Tanner Row B3
Terry Ave. C4
The Crescent A4
The Esplanade A2/B2
The Mount A4
The Stonebow C2
Toft Gn. A3
Tower St. C3/C4
Trinity La. B3
Victor St. B4
Walmgate D3
Wellington Row B2
Wellington St. C1
Willis St. D4

The Channel Tunnel

The Channel Tunnel is three tunnels, each 31 miles (50 km) long. The two outer tunnels carry railway tracks, one each way, with a connecting service passage between.

Eurotunnel manages the train operation called *Le Shuttle*. Slip roads from the M20 near Folkestone and the A16 near Calais, take cars direct to the terminals. Passengers pay at a toll-booth, go through frontier controls and load their cars onto the special carriages. The crossing itself takes about 35 minutes, but the whole journey, including Customs, embarkation and disembarkation, should take about an hour. There are four trains every hour at peak times, down to one an hour at quiet times. Food, drink and duty-free goods are on sale at the terminals, but not on on the train itself. Each carriage is air-conditioned and sound-proofed, and has access to a toilet and an information screen. The *Le Shuttle* Customer Service Centre is at Cheriton Parc, Folkestone - telephone 0990 353535.

Channel Ferry Ports

BELGIUM

Ramsgate - Oostende
Sally Ferries, up to 6 per day.
Felixstowe - Zeebrugge
P&O European Ferries, up to 2 per day.

FRANCE

Dover - Calais
P&O European Ferries, up to 25 per day.
Stena Sealink, up to 22 per day.
Hoverspeed Hovercraft, up to 14 per day.
Folkestone - Boulogne
Hoverspeed Seacat, up to 6 per day.
Newhaven - Dieppe
Stena Sealink, up to 4 per day.

Poole - Cherbourg
Brittany Ferries, up to 2 per day.
Portsmouth - Caen
Brittany Ferries, 3 per day.
Portsmouth - Cherbourg
P&O European Ferries, up to 4 per day.
Portsmouth - Le Havre
P&O European Ferries, up to 3 per day.
Ramsgate - Dunkerque
Sally Ferries, 5 per day
Southampton - Cherbourg
Stena Sealink, up to 2 per day.

HOLLAND

Harwich - Hoek van Holland
Stena Sealink, 2 per day.

Channel Ferry Ports

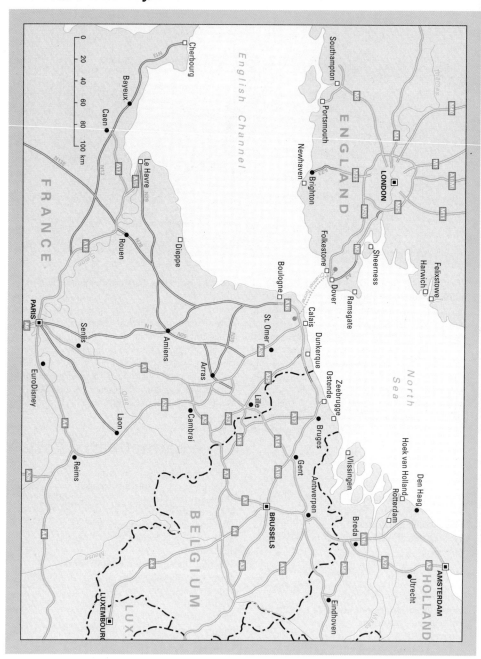